Nostradamus
The End of the Millennium

NOSTRADAMUS

THE END OF THE MILLENNIUM

PROPHECIES
1992-2001

V.J. Hewitt and Peter Lorie

Simon and Schuster

New York London Toronto Sydney Tokyo Singapore

SIMON AND SCHUSTER
Simon & Schuster Building
Rockefeller Center
1230 Avenue of the Americas
New York, New York 10020

SIMON AND SCHUSTER and colophon are registered trademarks
of Simon & Schuster Inc.

NOSTRADAMUS - THE END OF THE MILLENNIUM
was produced by Labyrinth Publishing S.A., Switzerland
Art direction and design by Malcolm Godwin

Typesetting by Dorchester Typesetting Group Ltd,
Dorchester, U.K.

Printed and bound by Mohndruck GmbH, Germany

10   9   8   7   6   5   4   3

Library of Congress Cataloging-in-Publication Data

Hewitt, V.J.
    Nostradamus : the end of the millennium : prophecies,
    1992-2001/ V. J. Hewitt and Peter Lorie.
            p.   cm.
    ISBN 0-671-74446-1
    1. Nostradamus, 1503-1566. Prophecies.   2. Prophecies
    (Occultism)
    I. Lorie, Peter.   II. Title.
BF 1815.N8H49 1991
133.3--dc20
                                                91-8761
                                                CIP

C O N T E N T S

INTRODUCTION
The Fire of Vulcan – Introducing and understanding the code. *(6)*

SECTION ONE
BRIEF EXPLANATION OF DECODING METHOD *(12)*

SECTION TWO
Into the Eighties – Using the system. *(15)*

SECTION THREE
Towards 2000 *(42)*

SECTION FOUR
THE FUTURE – EUROPE AND THE MIDDLE EAST *(49)* – Germany in Europe – France: Paris, Danger by Night – Britain in Europe – Fraud Destroys Swiss Financial System – Spain - The Basques and Gibraltar – Turkey Wars with Greece, Saddam Hussein. THE MIDDLE EAST *(68)* – Israel Defeated. NORTH AMERICA *(72)* – The California Earthquake Predictions – California Clawed Up – Mass Evacuation – San Diego Disappears – Giant Waves Hit Mexico – Los Angeles Undermined – San Francisco Devastation – After the Earthquake – America Burns – Space Craft Crashes. WORLD FIGURES *(108)* – Thatcher Again – Mitterrand Government Accused – Richard Gere Abandons Hollywood – President Nelson Mandela – Fonda and Turner Before Senate. SCIENCE AND TECHNOLOGY *(122)* – Advanced Technology Saves the German Economy – *Siécles* Alters the Human Brain – Computers Calculate Chaos – Mission to Mars – Aliens Televised. RELIGION AND MYSTICISM *(136)* – New World Religion – Osho Rajneesh – Women Priests – AIDS in the Catholic Priesthood. HEALTH, DISEASE AND SOCIETY *(146)* – Sound Waves Kill Cancer – Reversing the Ageing Process – The Power of Genetics – Education. THE FAR EAST *(154)* – Hong Kong and China – China Survives Alone – Japan's Economy in Trouble. AFRICA *(164)* – AIDS from Africa – Refugee millions die in Sudan. AUSTRALASIA *(168)* – A Fight for Rights. SCIENCE AND ECOLOGY *(172)* A Poisoned Earth – A New Hole in the Ozone Layer – The Black Hole Explained.

SECTION FIVE
THE SYSTEM REVEALED IN FULL *(180)*

THE FINAL CODE *(200)*

I N T R O D U C T I O N

THE FIRE OF VULCAN

INTRODUCING AND UNDERSTANDING THE CODE

"Maitre, how do I begin to understand your prophecies?"

"First, you must destroy them."

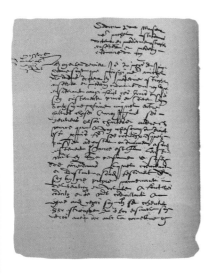

The handwriting of Michel Nostradamus.

WHEN THE MAN whom we know as Nostradamus was old, and knew that the great prophetic work that had occupied decades of his life was complete, he gathered together all his papers, notes, books and documents – records of a lifetime of secret prophecy – and burned them to ashes.

In the Preface to his prophecies, he writes that he offered them to Vulcan, the ancient Greek god who changed metals into weapons and tools. They burned with an extraordinary light, more brightly than might have been expected had they been ordinary documents, the flames illuminating his house as if it were a furnace.

Among the collection there were copies of centuries-old occult manuscripts and books, explaining ritualistic methods of calling up prophecy. These he also destroyed for fear of them falling into the wrong hands.

A few books and papers do not make the conflagration which Nostradamus describes. What else did he burn, or was it that he simply wanted us, his receiving descendants, to know that there was some great significance to this act of burning. Perhaps what we have today – those strange little verses known as "quatrains" – are not the real predictions at all. It may be that the papers he burned were the original and clear predictions which he had translated into the distorted form that we know today, in order that they might be disguised. Perhaps he recorded the act of burning simply to

draw attention to its significance. Nostradamus was not one to lightly discard an image. In fact, within the same Preface that he wrote, he tells us just this. He tells us that he condensed his original prophecies and wrote them in a twisted, obscure form to prevent the men of his time and future generations from knowing too much about how their world would change. The changes, he said, would be so great that these people would not comprehend his predictions until after they had happened. This prophecy is for sure correct!

Times have changed beyond all recognition between the period of Nostradamus' life and today. By contrast, a man from ancient Rome transported 1,200 years forward into the sixteenth century of Nostradamus would have found much that he could understand.

Latin and Greek were still spoken fluently by the educated. The Renaissance, based on the rediscovery of ancient Greek mathematics and astronomy, had just begun. Over a thousand years after Rome fell, animals and wheels were still the only source of transport.

But during the relatively short time – only 400 years – between Renaissance man and today, any visitor from the past would imagine that he had gone mad, or fallen into the clutches of demons! He would see people speeding about in cars, undertaking journeys of a few hours that in his time took weeks or months. He would see pictures, beamed into homes, of events taking place at that moment

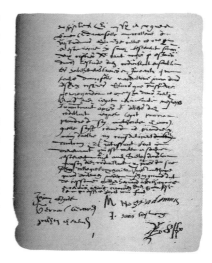

Above: A plaque commemorating the Prophet on the wall on the house in which he died on July 2nd 1566.

thousands of miles away. He would be told that within the space of sixty short years humanity had learned to fly and had landed on the moon, that people traveled to continents, unknown to him, in less than a day and that, while man was exploring other planets with machines, he was, at the same time, irreversibly damaging his own. And finally he would learn that the weapons man had developed were perfectly capable of annihilating the entire planet.

To realize that Nostradamus was this man – seeing all this extraordinary change from his home in old France – is to accept either that the whole idea is crazy, a fraud, or it is something that we need to give very serious thought to once more.

Yet, even in the twisted verses which are all he left to us, he gives the impression that he knew something of the changes occurring through the centuries to come. He describes situations that resemble, in part, historical events that have occurred since his day. Dramatic and vivid images scattered throughout his prophecies convey a feeling of changing society. Some of these images even call to mind the technology of the twentieth century – aerial combat, nuclear bombs, space travel. Yet every verse has a built-in distortion. There is no apparent continuity. It's a little like attempting to gauge the size and shape of objects in a room, looking through a deeply distorted mirror. At some point, and I think it was much earlier in his life than most other commentators believe, this prophetic genius set himself the monstrous task of drawing an entire planet into the light of a new day through the revelation of his power. Despite his gregariousness, there was a dark side to his character which betrayed the burden of a gift which he was unable to communicate fully to his own generation, but only to those living far distant in the future. We can fully understand such a problem. How could he have told his own people that in four hundred years' time human beings would be flying to the moon. They would simply have laughed!

We are the people to whom Nostradamus wanted to speak, the generation to whom he speaks clearly for the first time. We are the ones who will cross the invisible, but vital divide between one millennium and the next, between one age and another.

How could he do it? How could he prove to us, living four hundred years away from him, that the future could be accurately predicted?

First, he might have written his prophecies in a mixed-up fashion with just enough striking detail to keep generations fascinated by his words, until the time came when the key to them would be discovered again.

He knew that it *would* be rediscovered for he tells us so in a prophecy which we will examine in the last part of this book.

So what *did* Nostradamus destroy in his "Vulcan fire"? Surely it must have been the first prophecies that formed the basis for the twisted quatrains that we have today – the natural "ore" from which he crafted his fascinating and varied artifacts of prophecy. If they were destroyed, how can we ever know what they contained?

We must reverse the process by understanding what it was he intended, by "melting down" the verses we have until they reach

The signature of the Prophet.

Strangely there are virtually no portraits of Nostradamus although his fame stretched across France during his lifetime. This painting on the opposite page is the only known likeness.

once again the state that he first wrote them in.

What is needed is a method that will break up the quatrains and leave us with the raw material containing new, clear predictions that arise out of the old confused ones.

During the pages of this book the reader will learn a revolutionary new code and its application – will learn exactly how to take Nostradamus' verses and turn them back into the original prophecies – and also see how they can be applied with the most astonishing accuracy. This book, then, is a book of mysteries and marvels, telling the story of a quest, offering delights and fears, as well as the solutions to one of the most exciting riddles that history has ever offered.

The coding system is intended to be usable by anyone, and a complete explanation and proof of the system exists in the back of the book. A brief explanation also follows hereafter.

On the other hand, if the reader is simply willing to take the system on, then the bulk of the book is made up of direct and dated predictions on all manner of world-wide subjects. Maps, charts, diagrams and map references are provided so that there can be no doubt as to the precision of many of these prophecies. Not all will be successful. The authors are still learning. But it is anticipated that a high proportion of the coming future stories will be fulfilled, as the authors have already experienced sound proof of the decoding mechanism and its power for accuracy when compiling the book. Predictions actually came true as they were being written!

Last then, in this introductory chapter, we take a brief look at the code itself. If further clarification or proof is needed, the reader should turn to the section entitled *The System Revealed in Full* at the back of the book.

SECTION ONE

BRIEF EXPLANATION OF DECODING METHOD

ESSENTIALLY, THE SYSTEM IS QUITE SIMPLE. Nostradamus' original quatrains were written in old French, or Provence. Some of the letters that made up the lines of the verses were ancient in form, now no longer used, such as "f" instead of "s". In addition, the old spelling is often different to modern French. The first task of the decoder is to substitute the old letters for modern ones. But, and this is of fundamental importance, we do not discard the old letters (except in the case of the "f" to "s" which is merely a change of style). We simply raise it above the line – for example:

> *Le l*^y*on* **i**eune le vieux f*urmontera,*
> *En champ bellique par f*ingulier duelle,*
> *Dans cage d'or les yeux lu***y** crev**e**ra,*
> *Deux cla*ff*es* **v**ne puis mourir mort cruelle.*

Apart from the obvious "f" versus "s" letters, which serve no purpose within the decoding system, we can see the old French/Provence spelling, for example, **ieune/young** is spelled nowadays as **jeune. Luy/him** is now lui.

The first task then, is to unlock the coded texts by modernizing the verse without losing the essential elements.

We change the medieval "f" to "s" and we correct some of the more outlandish spellings by putting the familiar letters in.

As we shall see in the coming pages of prediction, each verse retains the raised letters above the line as these "left-over" letters are going to show us how to date the prophecy.

And now begins the real fun! The next stage is to treat the prose story we find as a potential anagram. The words are literally placed in a melting pot of anagramatical change. Using various rules, as can be seen at the end of the book in the section entitled *The System Revealed in Full*, the prophecy transforms, not simply into **one** prediction, but into many different predictions, all arising out of the first and original verse. The result is an extraordinary series of events, all connected through space and time, and all resulting in precise and often awe-inspiring predictions. The prophecies are seen to move from the past, through the present into the future.

The letters above the lines are then isolated, together with the substituted letters within the lines and a numerical code is applied – each letter of the alphabet having an equivalent number – a=1, b=2, c=3 etc. etc. – giving us, in each case, the day, month and year of the prediction. This information can be found with each prediction under the heading "Time-Signal".

So to begin the book with some sense of order in time, and to provide some additional help with the system, we will move slowly, starting with the recent past – taking verses that have been proven true by events – and then, with the same verses we will also move subtly and surprisingly into the future.

The chains which, supposedly, held the Apostle Peter during his imprisonment in Rome. Serious doubts are now cast upon the authenticity of such holy relics as it has been proved, not only that Peter was never in Rome, but also, that the "Rock of the Church" may never have actually existed at all. Leaders of the early Christian sects were all called Peter. It would appear that Nostradamus knew that his prediction of the discovery of the tomb would open up all the troubles of a Pandora's box instead.

SECTION TWO

INTO THE EIGHTIES

USING THE SYSTEM

APPLYING THE RULES set for decoding the prophet, we can become prophets ourselves and make our own deliberations about any time in this coming decade, simply by working through the quatrains. In the coming pages we take a look through the eighties and into the early nineties, choosing a single quatrain that ranges across the most important issues of this last decade and into the next — issues that will continue to unfold through to the end of this millennium.

Nostradamus' quatrains contain the most extraordinary subtlety insofar as they seem to create a whole story in time and space which would appear quite impossible to see in such detail, even if we were present ourselves at the events, let alone years in their past. But in this section – *Into the Eighties* – we find yet another wonder. Once we start to melt down the verses and look behind the surface, they seem to glide, almost imperceptibly, from descriptions of our recent past into those of the future. It is as though Nostradamus was on a roller coaster of time, unable to resist the events that appeared beside the tracks as he sped by. We, the witnesses of his gift, watch the words and letters of a single prophecy somehow melt into a system and then emerge again and again in descriptions of exciting, earth-moving and often tragic events — events that we have watched unfold in recent years. We then see these same events develop through an ever-moving present into the near and more distant future. It is as though Nostradamus lived them all and simply invites us to do the same — as, of course, we shall.

To give an example of how this works, and to provide the source of this coming section of the book, we can examine a familiar single

Above: The recently discovered tomb was believed to have been that of St. Peter. When Constantine had founded the first Church in Rome it is thought that he removed the saint's bones from his original grave to protect them from deterioration and possible grave robbers. He then placed them in this secret hiding place.

quatrain taking it through the system explained at the back of the book to reveal some of the *many* predictions it contains. We start with the quatrain itself and the well-known modern interpretation of it – one which we already know something about – but by using the new system we can first bring fresh information to bear, keeping in mind what we learned in the first chapter, and then seeing how the same prophecy examines several separate events in different times once we begin to melt it down. We start with the papacy.

The basic verse or quatrain is number III.65, and this is where the story starts –

> *Quand le fepulchre du grand Romain trouné,*
> *Le iour apres fera efleu Pontife,*
> *Du Senat gueres il ne fera prouvé,*
> *Empoisonné, fon fang au facré fcyphe*

Using the decoding system we can firstly "modernize" the verse from its archaic form and also solve the distorted riddles in Line 2. As shown, we retain the archaic letters for dating –

> **n**
> *Quand le sepulchre du grand Romain trouvé,*
> **i**
> *Aprés le jour sera Pont suée fiel*
> **u**
> *Il ne sera prouvé, du Senat guères,*
> *Sacré scyphe empoisonné au son sang.*

And in modern English we find –

"When the tomb of the great Roman is found, after a day a Bridge will be sweating gall. It will hardly show. Not long of the Senate, the 'sacred chalice' is poisoned by his own blood."

The prophecy in its "normal" format is concerned with events which occurred between August and September of 1978. Albino Luciani was elected Pope John Paul I on 26th August 1978 following only one day's debate by the Conclave of Cardinals. By September 29th he was already dead. The official cause was a heart attack John Paul only survived thirty days as Pope and yet in that all too brief time he endeared himself to the people as being a simple, compassionate and above all a true reformer.

but no death certificate was issued and no autopsy performed, leading to gossip that he was either murdered or committed suicide.

Nostradamus' description is precise – Pope John Paul I was killed by a condition in which his blood was poisoned by a rupture of the bile duct – "a sweating gall". The condition is also known as "uremia". ". . .the sacred chalice. . ." is ". . . poisoned by his own blood". However, this is not new to anyone who has examined Nostradamus' quatrains before. But if we take the quatrain through the complete meltdown process, something quite new begins to be revealed. Using the same letters of the modern French prophecy III.65, we place them into an anagramatical "pot", leaving out only those letters that we have selected to ask the question of the quatrain – i.e. if we want to know about the Pope, we withdraw the letters making up the word "Pope". Using the information gained from each of the separate lines of the verse to help us we produce a new prophecy from these remaining letters. The original raised letters remain in their original positions above the new letters.

The prose prophecy that results is made up of the letters in the original verse III.65, except for those new letters immediately below the raised letters that we added, and of course the letters that we used to ask the question. These new letters have been inserted into the text, using the information Nostradamus gave us in the hidden predictions for each separate line and keeping to one substitute letter per word. The system is therefore dependent essentially on anagram, with only one area of intuition – that of deciding what letters can be used as the substitute letters, those below the archaic letters that we have raised above the line. The choice of these substitute letters is made according to the sense of the prediction. This ability comes with practise. Having completed this anagram and letter substitution, we find the story begins to be revealed. For further and deeper explanation of this vital part of the decoding system, go to the last section of the book, where greater opportunity to practise the system is available.

       q   **u**   **n**   **o**
Paul F coeur rasé d'arthrite, or Jean Paul I meurt
         n   **s**   **n**   **g**   **u**   **s**   **r**
d'uraemia, conduit de la bile cassé au temps de s'election.
     s   **y**   **p**   **h**
"Venise" ne sera prouvé guère sang empoisonné.

Previous page: On August 25th 1978. Pope John Paul I, seated on his papal throne, carried by twelve attendants, is joyfully acclaimed by over 15,000 worshippers who attend his weekly audience.

Above: The previous, pious but strictly orthodox pope Paul had failed to win the hearts of many of his flock. John Paul, on the other hand, had captured their affection and it was with shocked disbelief that the news of his untimely death was discovered.

And in modern English we find –

"Paul VI's heart destroyed by arthritis, but John Paul I dies of uremia, the bile duct ruptured at the time of his election. "Venice" will hardly show poisoned blood."

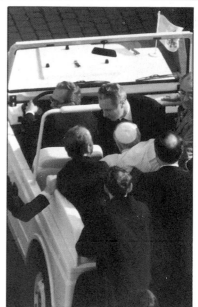

John Paul II was shot in Rome by a terrorist, Mehmet Ali Agca, who promptly declared he was the reborn Christ. Many, including the pope, believe the plot had been encouraged by the U.S.S.R.

The letter "F" in the first line has a numerical value of 6. Paul VI died on 6th August of a heart attack during a severe bout of arthritis, but Nostradamus still insists that his successor died of uremia and that this condition was not apparent until it was too late. John Paul I is referred to as "Venice" because he was formerly Patriarch of Venice.

The body of the dead pontiff is
carried across St. Peter's square
towards the Basilica, only thirty days
after his triumphal consecration.

Using these same letters and the same prophecy we begin now
to notice how the prediction drifts forward in time as we use the
complete meltdown system once again, taking all the letters of the
prophecy and our knowledge gained from the line-by-line method
to help us. We find ourselves next in 1981:

n

En Roman — ou songe, dupe d'un Russie qui rouvre son haine sur

e   c   n   o

URSS, US; Mehmet Ali Agca tire Karol, Jean Paul, des foules à la Place

n   g   y

de St. Pierre. Le pape survie.

In modern English —

"In Roman — where he dreams — he is fooled by the Russian
who revives his hatred of the USSR and the US; Mehmet Ali Agca
shoots Karol, John Paul, from among the crowds in St. Peter's Square.
The Pope survives."

On May 13th 1981, John Paul II, formerly Karol Wojtyla,
was shot by a terrorist, Mehmet Ali Agca in St. Peter's Square
who fired from among the crowds. The Pope always believed that there was a Russian influence behind the attempted
assassination.

Still on the same prophecy and once again, asking a different
question, continuing the meltdown process by producing another
anagram, we can now see how the bridge between past and future
is beginning to be made —

s   uu   n   e   u

Charles, Prince de Wales, épouse sa légère Diana Spencer au temple

u   o   s   s

de St.Paul. Deviendra reine qui joint son roi songeur en rouvrir

y   p

monarchie fugace.

Diana Spencer and Charles, Prince of Wales. Not only has Lady Di enlivened a royal image which has become rather dull and tweedy, she has had an equally striking effect upon a rather serious and retiring husband.

In English –

"Charles, Prince of Wales, marries his frivolous Diana Spencer at the temple of St.Paul. She will become a queen who joins her pensive king in reviving a fleeting monarchy."

Diana has already shown an ability to "liven" up the monarchy in England with her natural public relations abilities, though Nostradamus tells us the sovereignty of Charles will be brief.

The "Time-Signal" tells us a lot –

	u	o	s	s		s	y
Deviendra	*reine*	*qui*	*joint*	*son*	*roi songeur en rouvrir*		*monarchie*
			p				
			fugace.				
	20	14	18	18	18	23	15
	4	1:9	1:9	1:9	1:9	3	3
	2	5	9	9	9	5	6
	4	19	19	19	19	3	3
	2	May	9 (2)	9	9	May	
	Apr	91	91	91	91	3	9

24 is 42: Nostradamus predicts here and elsewhere that Prince Charles will take the British throne in 1991 when he is still 42 – the date at the bottom left indicates that Charles will be crowned on 2nd May 1992. 4:4 x 2 = 8. Prince Charles was born in 1948. (Don't forget that for Nostradamus this was very much in the future!)

Important years for Charles will be 1995, 1999 (two events), 1993 and 1998.

Mikhail Gorbachev will be remembered for his "glasnost" policies which culminated in the demolition of over a hundred miles of walls and electric fences which divided East and West Berlin by a ring of death.

Our next extraction from this same quatrain involves us in the life and times of Mikhail Gorbachev, starting in March 1985 and sliding forward as far as 1994:

>   **c**   **u**   **u**
> *Mikhail Gorbachev devient chef de URSS. Il permet l'Europe de*
>   **n**   **n**   **u**
> *l'est de renoncer à le passé. Joint un groupe qu'est sans rangs, or*
>   **a**   **u**
> *sans saper noyau – l'Europe.*

In English, this time, we find –

"Mikhail Gorbachev becomes leader of the USSR. He permits eastern Europe to renounce its past. It joins a group without ranks, but without undermining the nucleus – Europe."

The selection of remaining "upper" letters from our original quatrain, together with those below show us a time signal that indicates in 1992 there is a decision to allow the Eastern European countries into the European Community and that this will begin in 1994 after the 1st February.

Left: A Russian helicopter tests the levels of radioactivity.

Right: The official insignia for the Challenger mission. The tiny apple symbolizes the first teacher in space.

Moving slowly and inevitably forward in this Pandora's box of prophecy, all derived from one quatrain, we touch the future of nuclear power:

> **j**   **r**   **m**   **i**
> *Amerique: Navette spatiale Challenger explose à décoller.*
>   **o**   **n** **s**   **n**
> *URSS: Chernobyl réponse avec feux dans un réacteur.*
> **g**   **s**   **r**   **s** **p**
> *Vous guident au point où su ne dure pas.*

And the English –

> *"America: the space shuttle Challenger explodes on take-off.*
> *USSR: Chernobyl replies with fires in a reactor.*
> *They guide you to a point where knowledge fails."*

On January 26th 1986 the space shuttle Challenger blew up less than two minutes after it was launched and still climbing. Seven astronauts were killed and the NASA shuttle program was grounded.

Three months later, on 30th April, the number 4 reactor at the Chernobyl nuclear power plant in Russia caught fire. Nostradamus tells us that there was more than one fire. The top of the reactor was blown off and meltdown of the core seemed inevitable at one point. The result of this catastrophe is still not fully certain.

The dating to this prediction (not shown here) gives a clear indication of the future. Between 1995–6, knowledge and technology surrounding space travel fails the human race as it appears to have reached an impasse based on contemporary knowledge. Between 1996–8, a new era of science begins; some major new discovery which again involves space travel. The 7th March 1999 is a vital date in this sequence, relating to a revolutionary kind of technology which comes about through theories about how black holes function in the universe (See Science and Technology predictions in third section).

Next we come to one of the early warnings of perhaps the single most significant prediction of an event due to occur in the USA during this last ten years of the current century.

>   a   o   n
> *En California séisme de San Andreas que previent un jour noir*
>   s   a   c   s   c
> *Pour nations de l'Europe de l'est, le Mur est voie. Le vide attire*
>   y
> *peuples.*
> p   h
> *Se gausse d'un guru.*

In English —
"In California an earthquake from San Andreas that warns of a black day.
For the East European nations, the Wall is on the way. The vacuum attracts the peoples.
A guru is derided."

Almost three hundred people were killed in an earthquake which occurred in the San Francisco area of California on 19th October 1989. Movement in the San Andreas fault was responsible. The "black day" is that of the huge earthquake which is expected by the Californian people some time in the future. The 1989 quake was seen as a warning. In the next section we can examine the coming quake of 1993.

Calculations indicate that May 1993 is the date for this major earthquake. Just one month after the 1989 quake the Berlin Wall was breached, an event that this generation hardly expected to witness. The breach caused a political "vacuum" with the collapse of the Communist regimes in Eastern Europe. There is also a suggestion within this prediction of a mass migration of peoples from east to west, something which we are now seeing come about at time of writing from Russia and other Eastern European countries into Central Europe.

But a major migration can also be expected between August 1993 and May 1995. The "derided guru" seems to refer to Nostradamus himself, to whom the authorities do not pay sufficient attention.

Above: Buckled streetcar tracks in San Francisco 1906. *Left:* Buckled houses after the 1989 earthquake show the awesome and wrenching power of such a natural catastrophe.

Some of the most horrendous prophecies center upon a Middle Eastern scenario. Nostradamus mirrors the biblical predictions of an apocalyptic confrontation and locates Armaggedon, the legendary site of the ultimate battle of good against evil, in the region. Yet it appears that the gulf war of 1991 is to be the last major battle fought by U.S. troops and the marine who looks out towards occupied Kuwait in the early part of 1991 will be too preoccupied on the home front to take part in the final apocalypse.

And now we arrive at what may be considered the trickiest and yet most significant point of this book – the present! Because of the constraints of book publishing – preparation of manuscript, pictures, printing and binding – which can take almost six months to complete, the present for the writer is the past for the reader. The text for this book was prepared, edited and adjusted around the end of 1990, during the Christmas period, and prior to the January 15th deadline set by the United Nations for Saddam Hussein to withdraw from Kuwait. Final changes and adjustments were made on the text proofs in February of 1991 and during that short time some of the most significant events occurred with regard to the troubles in the Middle East. None of the following predictions or those in the future section on the Middle East were changed, each one continuing to be fulfilled as time made its inevitable mark.

> j c uu   o
> *Aprés Saddam Hussein envahie Kuwait, les Nations-Unis font*
> w   o   o   u
> *sanctions contre l'Iraq. Rat ronge péler. Leurre à promesse de guerre.*
> y   o
> *Fugue des peuples*

And the English version –

> *"After Saddam Hussein invades Kuwait, the United Nations make sanctions against Iraq. The rat gnaws to peel away. He deceives with a promise of war. The peoples run away."*

On the 2nd August 1990, Iraq invaded Kuwait and caused a global crisis. The world, through the United Nations, condemned Hussein and brought severe sanctions to bear on Iraq. Hussein threatened military retaliation on a huge scale and then positioned himself and his armies to fight a major war with the rest of the world – effectively this could be seen as a part of what Nostradamus might have enterpreted as the beginning of a Third World War. Seen from the distant past it would not be unrealistic to imagine that this planet has been permanently at war for the last two decades of the 20th century.

As on the previous page it is evident that absolute rulers have a penchant for creating edifices of themselves. Saddam Hussein has a particularily exhalted sense of his place in history. Here he is seen meeting the great 6th century ruler of fabled Babylon, Nebuchadnezzar. The mural on the right from Iran tells quite another story.

Nostradamus, in the above prediction, suggests that Hussein's actions are a bluff throughout the political maneuvering before the war began and indeed right up until the end of it, the desert rat "gnawing" all the time at his "cage" to find a way to gain what he wants – a small but rich part of Kuwait – and yet escape the power of the United States and the United Nations. His techniques have been those classically attributable to economic ambition in the hands of a dictator – diplomatic maneuvers and unpredictable, intractable behavior. Hundreds of thousands of foreign workers and their families have left Kuwait and Iraq, as Nostradamus predicted they would. The story continues in the Middle East section of the book. And in the meantime in Europe, we can take a look at the past/present/future predictions surrounding Germany's reunification.

p   v   i   p

Nulles, l'Allemagnes de l'ouest et l'est. Un pays que fera jour

u   g

nouveau en l'Europe. Sera résine à cordes en air doux. Europe à

s   h   c   p   h

rire non au sud. Gens sacrent.

"The Germanies of East and West are no more. One country which will make a new day in Europe. She will be the resin for the strings in a sweet tune. Europe will laugh, but not in the south. People curse."

As the economic power of the U.S.S.R. and its Eastern allies continues to disintigrate so hunger and homelessness become a nightmare. A unified and economically sound Germany increasingly finds herself as leader of the whole of Europe.

Nostradamus was quite adamant about the good that a unified Germany would bring – acting like "resin for the strings in a sweet tune" – very typical of his lyrical style with prophecy. Ultimately the whole of Europe will laugh, except for some cursing in the south. We may assume that this comes from the southern European countries such as Italy, which has recently spent much energy on pushing matters through with monetary policy – the Italian minister for Europe, Gianni de Michelis – who provoked Margaret Thatcher's crisis in late 1990. We may yet still see further problems from Spain, Italy and Greece. Predictions in the next section which relate to the later 1990s will show more detail to come.

The time-signal indicates that by 1995 Germany will have achieved her true role within Europe, the production of a "sweet tune" being the result. Between 1992-5 conditions in the south grow more troubled and by 1998 the European situation is not so happy, as we will see later in the book.

This one quatrain – III.65 – has revealed all that we have read so far in this section – taking us from the past through the ever-moving present into the future. But this is only a selection of what is available. Using this revolutionary new method of interpreting Nostradamus we can literally open new doors to the life that he prophesied - an almost unlimited picture. We have not included predictions that also arise from the system, directly within this one quatrain, related to the Iranian Revolution, the Iran-Iraq war, the IRA attempts to assassinate Margaret Thatcher, the Armenian earthquake, the recent changes in communism in Albania, the

Lockerbie air disaster in Britain. These can be drawn by any reader who cares to go deeper into the method provided, as can, of course, extensions of these past predictions and their "drift" forward into the future.

We can make a prediction through space — from one country into another — and through time — from one century into another. In this sense, provided we ask the right questions, the quatrains are like a written oracle. And what is perhaps most miraculous is the fact that we can achieve an almost unlimited number of interpretations from one single quatrain — once we know the date when it begins — and we can achieve the date by analyzing the letters above the line which Nostradamus left in the text to help us. (Further clarification of this method can be found at the back of the book)

As a final example for the end of this transition chapter, we can take one more interpretation close to the true starting point – the indicated date – of the quatrain number III.65 – July 1969 – giving us a startling piece of information that will guide us far into our own future –

> r   n   u   u   v   p
> *Dieu Apollo envoie Neil Armstrong a la lune. Utilise une*
>   o   g   u   a   r
> *technologie que se fanera. Série d'accidents serre NASA. Je prophétise*
>   s   s
>   *un systeme plu, pur, dur*

"The god Apollo sends Neil Armstrong to the Moon. He uses a technology which will fade. A series of accidents grips NASA. I prophesy a more successful, purer and tougher system."

During the next decade, space travel for the human race will be of major importance. According to Nostradamus, the method of traveling in space will be different from the one undertaken by NASA when Neil Armstrong commanded Apollo 11 to the moon in 1969. This prophecy directly predicts that there will be a reassuring change ("plus/plu" means "more/successful") which will enable mankind to travel more readily in space.

The time-signal indicates that the new technology will begin to emerge in 1992, bearing fruit for new space missions in 1998 and 1999. Once again it appears to be connected with a new form of physics created by fresh knowledge related to the theories surrounding black holes (see next section).

Using this method there should no longer be any problem with the previously rather "jerky" and vague interpretations made by various writers and interpreters of Nostradamus. The system provided here is natural, even sensuous in its fluid simplicity. Every quatrain possesses this capability – lacking the previous incoherence and fragmentation and containing an almost imperceptible "gliding forward" effect, from year to year and into the future, that we will now begin to sample in the next section.

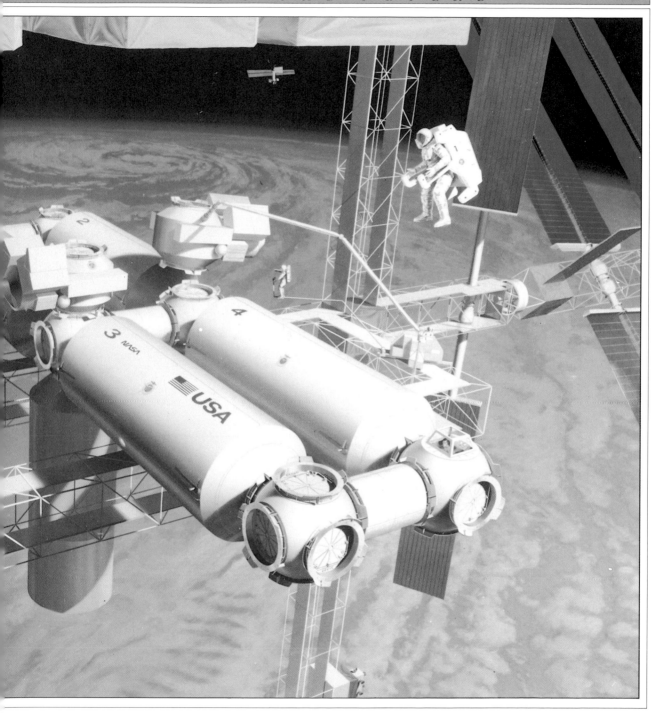

SECTION THREE

TOWARDS 2000

I N THE LAST SECTION we began the bizarre task of moving from the past, through the present and quite timidly into the future. The de-coding system set out in brief at the beginning of the book and complete at the end is the mathematics of the affair, but in section two we began to see how lyrical the device becomes when we put it to the test. It is as though we are using the art of a wizard – one who not only employs logic but also romance for his genius – the true craft of wizardry. Our predictions have invariably started in our past and moved forward into the future – like setting sail in a boat, we have found a suitable tide that runs our way and we have lifted our sails to a fresh breeze, ready to go, and yet we are still tied to the jetty with mooring ropes.

In order to slip those ropes and move out into the tide of the future, we must apply a simple additional method.

As the reader will have noticed, the dating system works largely, so far, on the basis that we know the dates that are being predicted. We can prove our system so long as we know where we are going. This may sound contradictory until we remember that the only purpose of working on the system up until now, has been to prove that it works – to build confidence in our ability to take the next step forward. Thus, in events that have not yet taken place, in the future, this system inevitably breaks down – or does it? Nostradamus, in fact, encoded a method of looking cleanly at the future, within the quatrains that he wrote and we shall see in this section how this works and how to apply it.

What arises out of the discoveries that we are about to make in this next section is that Nostradamus had a special place in his heart for the last ten years of the 20th century. As though there were some special significance to this era, almost all of the quatrains in the "Siécles" (Nostradamus' life work was entitled "Siécles" – in

As our present world seems to come to an end Nostradamus predicts that major institutions, like the Catholic Church, will lose support and credibility and will have become extinct by the end of the millennium. He sees the present pope as dying by 1995 and agrees with the 12th century prophet, Malachi, that there are only two popes left in the succession before the final fall of the Church of Rome.

English "The Centuries") seem to reveal material which effectively stops between the years 1991 and 2001! It is as though these years were the culmination of his most important message. All hitherto interpretations of the prophet's works have effectively been erroneous – the result of Nostradamus' determination to keep us all interested in his words until the right time arrived and the proper decoding system was discovered – that time has finally come and we can take full advantage of what he intended us to see.

Much is spoken about the end of the world coinciding with the last year of the 20th century. We seem to associate catastrophe with millennium ends – the last millennium end saw similar predictions and forecasts but, of course, nothing of the kind occurred. We seem to imagine that the forces of the universe that would be responsible for the end of a planet are interested in the dates that we have ascribed to our lives. What does existence care about the year 2000? It is only our own minds that make these assumptions. In any case, Nostradamus' predictions show a keen interest in a new religion that begins in the 21st century and takes mankind through a thousand years of peace and happiness. If we believe the prophet then we can look forward to a delightful future! The times of strife are now, not next century!

In a sense, though, our present world is coming to an end. Climatic factors are changing the physical world, social factors are altering our environment, technology is altering the scientific world, major institutions such as the Catholic Church will die in the next few years. One age is slipping away and another age coming into force – perhaps it is a new age, perhaps only another age that we can see as a repeat of a much older one that we thought had died.

In order to set sail out into the free breeze of the future, we have selected five prophecies. All the future predictions associated with the next ten years will be drawn from these five quatrains, worked in the manner that has been explained hitherto. We could have selected virtually any of the quatrains from "Siécle", there is no special magic about these five, except that they have been worked on by the authors and are therefore more familiar.

1.35 –

   y i

Le lion jeune le vieux surmontera,

   En champ bellique par singulier duelle,

    y u

Dans cage d'or les yeux lui crevera,

    v

   Deux classes une puis mourir mort cruelle.

1.42 –

   u

Le dix Calende d'Avril de faict Gotique,

   Resuscité encor par gens malins,

Le feu estainct, assemble diabolique,

   Cherchant les os du d'Amant et Pielin.

III.65

        n

Quand le sepulchre du grand Romain trouvé,

  i

   Le jour apres sera esleu Pontife,

                    u

Du Senat gueres il ne sera prouvé,

   Empoisonné, son sang au sacré scyphe.

X.22

               u

Pour ne vouloir consentir au divorce,

   Qui puis apres sera cogneu indigné,

  y

Le Roi des Isles sera chassé par force

       y

   Mis à son lieu qui de Roi n'aura signe.

X.74

   u

An revolu du grand nombre septiesme,

       i

   Apparoistra au temps jeux d'Hecatombe,

Non esloigné du grand eage milliesme,

   Que les entrez sortiront de leur tombe.

Two of these verses – I.35 and III.65 appear in the first and last sections of this book. The other three are new treasure-troves for us to begin working on.

We are not going to interpret the three new verses at this point as our concern in the coming pages is for the future, and the future will arise out of the collection of letters that each verse holds. We can mention that verse I.42 has been previously identified with the introduction of the Gregorian Calendar in 1582 and verse X.22 with the abdication of Edward VIII in 1936. These are only the starting points in history of the two prophecies – the beginning of our treasure hunt – for once we know the mechanism that makes them move through time, i.e. that of asking the question of the quatrain by removing the relevant letters, then we can begin to take our steps forward along the most fascinating part of the journey.

The four verses then – I.42, X.22, I.35 and III.65 – will provide us with the basis for all the general predictions that we map out in the coming sections of the book about the future. All of them began at points in our past and can be moved forward through the coming years by the methods already explained.

However, the fifth verse – X.74 – is different. This verse begins its journey into the future from a starting point which is *still in* our future – the California Earthquake of 1993.

These five verses are capable of yielding up a massive amount of information on a great variety of subjects. We are only able to sample a very small selection in this book. We shall be seeing well-known names and places – people that we see regularly on our television screens, places that we read about in our newspapers. But these people and places will turn up in situations – under circumstances – that we have not yet experienced! The descriptions will be surrounding situations that have not yet occurred – the politics, economics, social developments and technological, scientific discoveries of the future – a time we do not know.

The precise starting point of the fifth verse we described above – X.74 – is just a little time before the California Earthquake in 1993. Its true starting point is the American and European celebrations that will take place in 1992 – the five-hundredth anniversary of the discovery of North America in 1492 by Christopher Columbus. And in the same way as Columbus set sail with a small fleet into the unknown, we are about to do the same – letting go the mooring ropes to sail out into the future.

SECTION FOUR

THE FUTURE

EUROPE – GERMANY

"Germany in Europe" – 1991-1994

Drawn from verse III.65

January 1991 Revellers celebrating
the unification of the two Germanies.

> in   h   o   m
> *L'Europe sera changé par l'Allemagne unifiée. / Trouvera que la*
> p   o   s   o   s n
> *sente d'or dure/à URSS. Fer à sud./Peuple songe à nouvel âge sur*
> y   u   j
> *en espace. Desirent science.*
>
>
> *"Europe will be changed by a united Germany. She will find that
> the golden path stretches to the USSR: an iron one in the south.
> People dream of a new and certain age in space. They want the
> science."*

January 1991 Revellers celebrating
the unification of the two Germanies.

NB – the / lines in the French verses indicate the breaks that
correspond to the time-signal breaks. For a full explanation of the
system and the following time-signals, please turn to the back of
the book – "The System Revealed in Full".

Time-Signal

i	n	h	o	m	p	o	s	o	s	n	y	u	j
a	c	e	e	e	e	a	f	l	l	g	e	e	e
1:9	13	8	14	12	15	14	18	14	18	13	23	20	10
1	3	5	5	5	5	1	6	11	11	7	5	5	5
19	4	8	5	3	6	5	9	5	9	4	5	2	1
1	3	5	5	5	5	1	6	2	2	7	5	5	5
	194	8	May		9	95		95				92	
191	3		Oct	May	5	1 June							
						May		2	Feb	Dec 11			
						1 96							

EUROPE WILL CHANGE for the better between 3rd October 1991 and 8th May 1994 by the unification of Germany – Nostradamus indicates that this is beyond doubt. The change will inevitably create a "golden path" all the way to the borders of the Soviet Union, a shining future of peace, prosperity and scientific innovation in May 1995.

At the same time another path of "iron in the south" between 1st June 1995 and 1st May 1996 is being forged with troubles afflicting the Mediterranean, southern European countries of Italy and Greece. Other predictions verify this.

Between 11th December 1992 and 2nd February 1995 there will be "dreams" of a new space age. By "dreams" Nostradamus refers to revolutionary theories arising from "right-brain" intuition imposing themselves on the stale outmoded thinking of "left-brain", standard technological processes. (See Science and Technology predictions)

The ways of the more introverted "new age" thinking that will arise in the next years may well also contribute to this new science.

The Brandenburg gate has been the symbol of division of East and West ever since the wall was erected in 1961. Unarmed and relaxed East German soldiers line the wall as West Berliners mingle with the East for the first time in 30 years.

"Paris – Danger by Night" – 1991-1995

Drawn from verse X.22

      i   i

Dans le cité de Paris, groupes des voyous errent / par

  i   i   o i   o a

les rues / commes loups, cognent ceux qui se hasardent / en

      i   y   r i   n

soir, un force grisé que / nie la vie aux autres.

"In the city of Paris, bands of young thugs roam the streets like wolves, beating up those who take risks in the evening, a drunken force which denies life to others."

Time-Signal

| i | i | i | i | o | i | o | a | i | y | r | i | n |
e	t	s	m	t	x	t	e	e	e	e	x	t
1:9	1:9	1:9	1:9	14	1:9	14	1	1:9	23	17	1:9	13
5	19	18	12	19	22	19	5	5	5	5	22	19
19	19	19	19	5	19	5	1	19	5	8	19	4
5	19	9	3	19	4	19	5	5	5	5	4	19
							Jan			5	Aug	194
195	1991	199	193	195	194	195	5	195	May	5		194

DURING 1991–95 PARIS becomes a lawless city at night, terrorized by bands of youths who threaten the French capital's famed night life. 1992 is not included which may indicate a crackdown by the authorities which has no lasting effect. The year 199 (normally 1999) does not fit into the series and may refer to 19th September 1991 or 1993.

An incident involving drunken violence is highlighted on 5th January 1995.

Either actual loss of life occurs during the period from 5th May to 5th August 1994, or Nostradamus is referring to a curfew which results in Paris becoming a dead city at night. If so, this initial period may be extended to cover the whole of 1994.

"Britain in Europe." – 1992–1996

Drawn from verse III.65

f   g
Le Royaume-Uni se trouvé partie d'une grande alliance
n   j   s
de l'Europe: / souverainetés / des nations perdu. /
e   u   a   g
An l'espace atmosphérique / personnes choir sur US.

*"The United Kingdom finds itself part of a great European alliance;
the sovereignty of each nation lost.
In a year of outer space, people will fall on the USA."*

Time-Signal

f t	g e	n e	j t	s d	e a	u i	a e	g i
6	7	13	10	18	5	20	1	7
19	5	5	19	4	1	1:9	5	1:9
6	7	4	10	9	5	2	1	7
19	5	5	19	4	1	19	5	19
196	7	Apr	91:10		5	192	1	197
	May	5	2001	94	Jan		May	

THE UNITED KINGDOM, which did not exist in Nostradamus' lifetime, is, at present, being swept along in the irresistible tide of events unfolding in Europe. This process will surely accelerate. It will have reached a crucial stage during the period between 7th April and 5th May 1996, indicating that European monetary and economic union will be achieved by that stage.

During the years 1991–2001 the sovereignty of all nations will be lost in the formation of this great European alliance, including, perhaps, some, if not all republics from the Soviet Union. Europe

The "Iron Lady", Margaret Thatcher, in characteristic battle mood. This latter-day Queen Boudicea has fought to retain British sovereignty and currency in a Europe which seeks to have more common aims. Nostradamus clearly indicates that national pride and interests will be swept aside by the wider considerations of a Super-Europe.

Thatcher, from her first year to her resignation as Prime Minister of the U.K. has always assumed almost heroic status. The British Sunday Times wryly captures this Joan of Arc-like quality in both her first year of glory and her final martyrdom in 1990.

THE SUNDAY TIMES *magazine*

HER FIRST YEAR

will have seen nothing like it since the fall of the Roman Empire 1,600 years ago.

The year when this great decision will be made is 1994, already the target year for closer monetary union and a prominent factor in the causes leading up to Mrs. Thatcher's resignation in November 1990. (In another prediction, Nostradamus indicates that she will be re-elected leader of the Conservatives in 1995, but in opposition. Possibly this is a last-ditch, but futile, attempt to fight Britain's inevitable inclusion in the new super-Europe.) See WORLD FIGURES.

There are great achievements in space exploration during the year from 5th January 1992.

Turning to the space accident dated 1st May 1997, the non-sexual use of *personnes* may indicate that one or more astronauts are women.

A clue to the nationality of the spacecraft is located in the anagramatic

g

phrase: *choir sur US*

g   u

which becomes *Russie choir* – *"Russia will fall"*.

The spacecraft is Russian. 1st May is a day of national celebration in the Soviet Union as it is throughout Europe. The space mission may be timed to coincide with this date, but goes horribly wrong. (See AMERICA predictions.)

"Fraud Destroys Swiss Financial System."
— 1995

Drawn from verse X.22

      i   **r**   **c**   **i**

Pour quoi prouve La Suisse sa voracité / — non par direct

    n   **s**   **i**   **d**

cours du change, mais / en session illégale de fourberie que

     o   **i**   **y**

ruine / sa reputation, système d'argent?

"For what does Switzerland show her hunger — not through a direct rate of exchange, but in an illegal session of cheating that destroys her reputation and money system?"

Time-Signal

i	r	c	i	n	s	i	d	o	i	y
e	t	a	t	d	m	e	b	t	t	t
1:9	17	3	1:9	13	18	1:9	4	14	1:9	23
5	19	1	19	4	12	5	2	19	19	19
19	8	3	19	4	9	19	4	5	19	5
5	19	1	19	4	3	5	2	19	19	19
	198	Mar		Apr			Apr	195		195
195		1	1991	4	93	195	2		1991	

Increasingly Switzerland finds herself out in the economic cold surrounded by the increasingly stable currencies of the European partners. The once solid and certain stability of her own Swiss Franc had begun to appear vulnerable by the beginning of the last decade of the 20th century.

THE COMPLETE PREDICTION is phrased as a question, illustrating Nostradamus' opinion of the futility of this illegal activity, involving huge deception connected with the rate of exchange between Swiss francs and other currencies.

The deception is gradually uncovered between 1995-1998, but operates secretly between 1st March 1991 — 4th April 1993.

An important date in the detection process may be 2nd April 1995.

During 1995 Switzerland's financial reputation and consequently her wealth are destroyed, with the revelation of this secret fraud operating from 1991.

"Spain – The Basques and Gibraltar."
1993 – 2000

Drawn from verse X.74

Un rai de lumiére, les Basques, orthodoxes, anodins.

          m   **p**

L'indépendance un but. Roi Juan Carlos et le gouvernement

   g   **m m** **z** **l**   **t** **m**

d'Espagne misent le / sort de / Gibraltar en Europe.

"A ray of light, the Basques, orthodox, harmless, independence a target. King Juan Carlos and the Spanish government place the fate of Gibraltar in Europe."

Time-Signal

m	p	g	m	m	z	l	t	m
c	n	n	n	l	s	d	l	n
12	15	7	12	12	24	11	19	12
3	13	13	13	11	18	4	11	13
3	6	7	3	3	6	2	19	3
3	4	4	4	2	9	4	2	4
		97	3	Mar	96	2		193
Mar	4	10*				Apr	Feb	4

*Dating: 10 = AD 2000

Right: Masked Basque separatists hold a press conference. The reality of these fiercely independent peoples contrasts somewhat with Nostradamus's mild description of their being "*orthodox and harmless*".

Violent clashes on the streets with Spanish authorities are a frequent occurrence. Barricades like this will only cease when the Basques gain independence.

BY AD 2000 SPAIN WILL HAVE SOLVED two important problems – the demand of the Basque people for independence and the dispute with Britain over possession of Gibraltar.

The Basques of northern Spain are an ancient people with a record of fierce resistance against occupying powers, including the Romans. Their language is different from any other in Europe, going back to the Stone Age. During this century there have been bitter clashes between Basque separatists, spearheaded by the terrorist organisation ETA, and the Spanish authorities.

Following a decision to give them independence, the Basques will renounce violence.

No dating appears for the Basque prediction, indicating that the Spanish government will deal with both issues at the same time.

The second prediction relates to the long-running argument between Britain and Spain over possession of Gibraltar, the strategic base overlooking the entrance to the Mediterranean from the Atlantic.

Increasingly, the new European super-community will settle border disputes among its members and from 4th February 1993, Gibraltar may become a special European protectorate. After 2nd April 1996 Gibraltar's political fate will be determined, an important period in the process being 3rd March 1997 – 4th March 2000.

Britain and Spain may finally surrender Gibraltar to direct European rule, since it is too small to become independent. Whatever the outcome, the issue is settled by the turn of the century.

Note: although verse X.74 has mainly been identified in this book with predictions of the Californian earthquake, like all prophecies, it can produce predictions of other events.

"Turkey Wars with Greece – Saddam Hussein in the Middle East." – 1991 – 1998

Drawn from III.65

s   n   l   p
La Turquie, Grèce rouvrent la guerre, tandis qu'au sud
               p   s   i
la Chypre fêle. / S Hussein pousse notre pouvoir / fané à
s   o   j   p
l'écart. / Noue damier méditerranéen. Son, sang.

"Turkey and Greece reopen the war, while to the south Cyprus shatters. S.Hussein thrusts our fading power aside. He knots up the Mediterranean draughtboard. Noise, blood."

Time-Signal

s r	n t	l r	p q	p t	s i	i f	s l	o t	j i	p a
18	13	11	15	15	18	1:9	18	14	10	15
17	19	17	16	19	1:9	6	11	19	1:9	1
9	4	2	6	6	9	19	9	5	1	6
7	19	8	7	19	19	6	2	19	19	1
	194		8	196	199		9	195	191	6
97			July			196	2			Jan
		Aug								
		198	7							

It is difficult, at the time of writing, in early 1991, to see Saddam Hussein remaining in power and yet Nostradamus sees him as an ultimate survivor in some form or another. Even if he is personally eliminated his legend could well be used as a rallying focus for Arab and Palestinian unrest. Martyrs are often more useful to revolutionaries than leaders who are alive. Lenin must surely be a perfect example.

TURKEY AND GREECE go to war over the island of Cyprus, long a source of dispute, and at present partitioned between these two countries. The delicate balance of rule is shattered and Cyprus suffers severe damage, economic and material, from the outbreak of conflict. The relevant dates are 8th July 1994, 1997 and 7th August 1998.

As the first draft of this book was being completed, the world was locked in confrontation with Iraq over its invasion of Kuwait.

This prediction indicates that Saddam Hussein, the President of Iraq, survives the Gulf War, both physically and politically. The information given here should be linked with the "Israel Defeated" prediction (See MIDDLE EAST), which states that in a war with Iraq, Syria and Egypt, Israel will be defeated and overrun.

"S.Hussein thrusts our *fading power aside ..."*

As the descendant of Jews, although his family had converted to Roman Catholicism, Nostradamus identifies personally with the downfall of Israel, expressing a tacit sorrow. This personal identification also occurs in the MIDDLE EAST prediction referred to above. It is not stated that this is the end of the experiment which began with the recreation of the state of Israel almost 2000 years after it fell to the Roman sword, but it does look very much like it.

Saddam Hussein pursues his path to power in the Middle East between 1996–9. Israel's resistance begins to weaken after the period 9th February 1995 and 2nd September 1996.

The final part of the prediction might have been thought to have been a consequence of Hussein's growing victory over Israel, but the date tells us differently.

As the first draft of this text was completed it seemed, according to the primary dates in the time-signal, that Hussein might complicate the power structure in the Mediterranean on 6th January 1991. The UN had then just passed a resolution authorizing the use of force if Iraq had not withdrawn voluntarily from Kuwait by 15th January 1991.

The primary time-signal suggests that conflict would break out on or near the 6th January between Iraq and the powers ranged up against her over the invasion of Kuwait and then spill over into the Mediterranean. The last two words of the prediction convey better than most the impact of war.

Left: Turkey's President Ozal attempts to court the European Community and the U.S.A. while, at the same time, having to live with his Islamic neighbors. Turkey's long-standing emnity with Christian Greece, founded on grievances as long past as the Ottoman Empire, is always likely to erupt in non-rational ways. *Right:* Greek and Turkish Summit Conference held in June 1988. The two symbols of Cross and Crescent eloquently attest to the religious undertow of any relationship between the nations.

In the event, the Gulf War began on 16th January at a few minutes to midnight, British time, when Allied aircraft took off on the first of continuous bombing raids over Iraq.

And here is a perfect example for us to see the use of the Supplementary Dates, as, if we include them, the Dating System reveals this information –

Time Signal – Final Section

15	15th
1 ⎫	
6 ⎭	16th
1	January
191	1991

The phrase "he knots up the Mediterranean draughtboard" has also become more clear. A few days before the conflict began, tourists were told to leave holiday resorts, including Cyprus, at the eastern end of the Mediterranean. During the conflict, Iraq launched missiles at Israel inflicting damage on Tel Aviv and Haifa on the Mediterranean coast. American forces were also moved into Turkey as a precaution against Iraqi attack.

THE MIDDLE EAST

"Israel Defeated by her Arab Neighbors." 1995–1998

Drawn from verse III.65

>   u   o   m   o   o   r
> *Sans guet Amerique chaude Israel fait la guerre / contre les*
>   o   e   c   n   j   u s   s   u
> *Palestiniens. Un rond / de l'Egypte, Syrie, Irak est plus / fort pour*
>   p   h   s
> *nous. / Vannent à perte de / vue.*

"Without the sentry — 'hot' America — Israel makes war against the Palestinians. A circle of Egypt, Syria and Iraq is too strong for us. They winnow a wasteland as far as I can see."

Time-Signal

| u | o | m | o | o | r | o | e | c | n | j* | u | s | s | u | p | h | s |
t	e	i	e	t	s	i	r	t	y		t	l	f	o	t	t	u
20	14	12	14	14	17	14	5	3	13	10	20	18	18	20	15	8	18
19	5	1:9	5	19	18	1:9	17	19	23		19	11	6	14	19	19	20
2	5	3	5	5	8	5	5	3	4	10	2	9	9	2	6	8	9
19	5	19	5	19	9	19	8	19	5	1	19	2	6	5	19	19	2
192	5	193	5	195	98	195	5	193	4		192	9			196	198	92
May		May						Aug					Feb				
Feb 5		Mar 5						May					96 5				
195		195															

* There is no letter "K" in the French alphabet so that in our coding system it possesses no value, numerically.

THE INSERTION OF MANY SUBSTITUTE letters in the meltdown process of Nostradamus' verses seems invariably to indicate a sensitive subject. As we have seen before, Nostradamus has a personal identification with the Jewish peoples of Israel and brings himself into the prediction directly.

Below: An Israeli soldier with Hawk anti-aircraft missiles pointing over the Jordan valley. Israel depends largely upon the U.S. for the high-tech weaponry which keeps the balance of power in the region. However, the Arab nations which surround the tiny Jewish State might be able to overwhelm their neighbor with sheer numbers if there was enough provocation.

lam Hussein · Yasser Arafat · King Hussein · Hosni Mubarak · Hafez Assad

America, if we look again at the panoramic future history of the world, is very much occupied with her problems of agricultural depletion after the terrible droughts and the massive earthquake of 1993. According to the time-signal the loss of interest in her foreign policy, at least with regard to Israel, begins in the run-up to the earthquake – 5th May 1992 – 5th May 1993 and continues crucially between 5th February and 5th March 1995. This attitude also continues further into the decade.

Israel apparently takes this opportunity to attack her Palestinian Arab neighbors. According to the prophecy Israel's war continues between 1995 and 1998 and is not only concerned with the Arabs living in the West Bank, since she already occupies this territory, but with the Palestinian camps based in Syria and Iraq under such leaders as Yasser Arafat. In this case Syria and her neighbors would certainly enter such a war.

The prophecy states that the result of this decision is catastrophic for Israel as Egypt, Syria and Iraq form a circle around the country, probably cutting off her Mediterranean access.

The Arab alliance has been formed prior to the attack between 9th February 1992 and 4th May 1993. It holds until 5th February 1996 when Israel begins to lose the war – for, as Nostradamus states, her enemies are too strong. Between 1996 and 1998 Israel is devastated and presumably overrun by Arab armies. The last date – 1992 – seen at the right-hand end of the time-signal, is a final warning both to Israel and America that this grim prospect is "seen" by Nostradamus and perhaps could be avoided if noted by the authorities involved.

America's involvement with Saddam Hussein in Iraq and Kuwait must have a major bearing on the predicted war brought about by Israel. According to the predictions we have already seen and others that are yet to be included here, Hussein is still around in his leadership position into the mid-90s which suggests that his quest was not thwarted successfully during 1991.

This rather doomy prediction seems to suggest the end of the modern nation of Israel almost 1,900 years after the devastation it suffered at the hands of Rome.

A Palestinian girl runs past Israeli troops in Old Jerusalem, a gay butterfly of hope caught amongst drab military khakhi in 1990. By the time the next major conflict erupts in the region this girl, herself, could be a mother. What hope for any of the children of the region?

N O R T H   A M E R I C A
The California Earthquake Predictions

WE BEGIN THIS VERY SIGNIFICANT part of the book with a rather strange prophecy – one that does not reveal itself so readily as others so far. The following pages, though, will tell a remarkable story, one that alters the course of history if all or even some of these predictions are fulfilled – bringing the biggest single earthquake to hit the United States in its civilized history.

Unlike other verses in the book, before we get into the interpretation of this one we will take a brief look at the original verse itself, and then the method by which we decode this strange piece of prophecy.

Verse X.74

u

An revolu du grand nombre septiesme,

i

Apparoistra au temps jeux d'Hecatombe,
Non esloigné du grand eage milliesme,
Que les entrez sortiront de leur tombe.

"A completed year of the great number seven
It will appear during the Games of the Hecatombe
Not far from the great age-year
As you enter them they will come out of their tomb."

The subject does not immediately show itself, but the solemn tones of this prophecy sound a chilling note. What are the clues trailed by Nostradamus that lead to the revelation of its secrets?

Firstly the anagrams and word-games. The French word *revolu* means "completed", but is also a precise anagram for *louver* – meaning "claw up", a powerful, almost "revelatory" description for earth movements.

The French word *septiesme* has been distorted to indicate that it contains another word – in this case *seisme* – earthquake.

These first hints indicate the likely subject of the verse, and the tone of the prophecy indicates a major event. What, then, were the *"Games of the Hecatombe"*? *Hecatombe* is usually translated as "slaughter", but the term comes from the Roman festival in honor of Hecate, goddess of night and the underworld, or the realm of the dead. These Games were held in much the same way as our modern Olympic Games but with animal sacrifices to the goddess. Nostradamus' analogy, taking all the senses of the verse into consideration, is that this event is going to occur at the time of the next Olympic Games – "Not far from the great age-year" – the end of the millennium.

Spain, the host of the 1992 Games, is synonymous with bull-fighting, the slaughter of animals, and no place in Spain more so than Barcelona, where the Games will be held.

So the "completed year of the great number seven" could begin in 1992 and end in 1993 – *seven* years away from AD 2000 – "the great-age year."

If we then commence the melt-down process, taking the second line anagramatically, we find further information –

s   i

Roi apparait au temps jeux d'Hecatombe
"A King appears at the time of the Games of Slaughter."

Line two then becomes a reference to the Coronation of Charles III, the present Prince of Wales, in 1992.

The prophecy describes a period beginning in 1992 with the Coronation of Charles III and the Olympic Games in Spain and ending in 1993 with a great earthquake seven years away from the new millennium.

And then the last line –

"As you enter them, they will come out of their tomb."

Littered throughout Nostradamus' prophecies are statements in the "you" form – direct instructions to any interpreter who manages to understand them as such. This instruction says, "the more you enter into the codes and understand them, the more lives will be saved."

This brief beginning gives us enough of a starting point to delve deeper into the verse with some confidence. But now, what about the dating of the predicted event?

DATING THE QUAKE

In Lines One and Three are hidden codes.
Line One

u
An revolu du grand nombre septiesme

This is the complete line. To locate the date of the earthquake, remove the following phrase from the line

u
An revolu du grand séisme
louver
"A complete year clawed by a great earthquake".

The letters below are what remain of the line.

n	o	m	b	r	e	/	p	t	e
13	14	12	2	17	5	/ 15		19	5
4	5	3	2	8	5	/ 6		19	5
	9	3	2	8	5	/ 6 + 1 = 7		9 + 5 = 14 = 5	

Look carefully at these final numbers – they hold the key to the dating of the earthquake.

93   2   8 May (5th month)   7   5

The date and time that clearly emerges is –
8th May 1993 at 7:05

The earthquake is prophesied to happen on 8 May 1993 at 7:05. The number "2" indicates the scope of the whole prediction - the complete year would therefore be 2nd May 1992 – 8th May 1993. The letters "p", "t" and "e" come from the distorted *septiesme/seven*. It seemed natural to follow the sequence until 7 emerged. This is the *hour* of the earthquake. The sequence then

In this outline map of California and Western Nevada the shaded yellow area, which extends from Pahute Mesa in the north to Cabot Colonet in the south, shows the region of greatest seismic disturbance. The line stretching from the Juan De Fuca plate in British Columbia to the Peru-Chilean Trench in the south shows the front line where the Pacific Plates meet the land masses of North and South America. This uneasy region, which includes the San Andreas fault, is a zone of intense volcanic activity, having over 30 potentially active volcanoes along its leading edge. It is this clash of giants which creates the devastating quakes, eruptions and slides which have dogged the area for the last century.

Opposite: As the Pacific plate (shown as grey in the diagram) moves under the lighter American plate, huge explosive forces release energies greater than a thousand bombs of Hiroshima. Seismic waves from each cataclysmic scenario will rock the land and coastal seas with quakes well in excess of eight magnitudes.

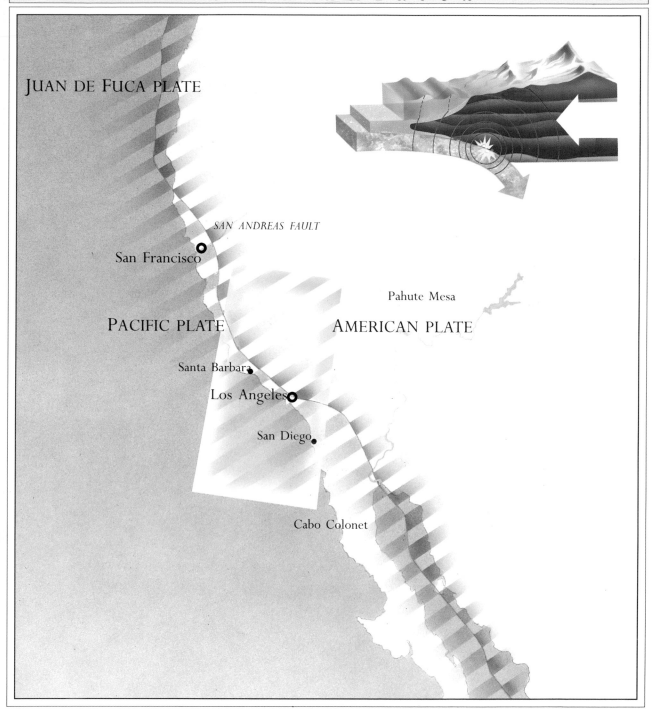

JUAN DE FUCA PLATE

SAN ANDREAS FAULT

San Francisco

Pahute Mesa

PACIFIC PLATE

AMERICAN PLATE

Santa Barbara

Los Angeles

San Diego

Cabo Colonet

produces 5 — the actual minute when the earthquake begins. This time is confirmed several times in the following predictions.

California is in the Pacific Time Zone — we can assume that Nostradamus is using Pacific time, not European time. The word "zone", appearing in the predictions, is a device indicating map co-ordinates, but he may also have employed it to confirm the local-time factor.

Whether it is 7:05 in the morning or evening, cannot clearly be deduced, but the reference to Hecate, goddess of night, death and the underworld might suggest that it is 7:05 p.m.

As the earthquake hits the seaboard cities the pent-up emotions of many underprivileged groups could well explode. The heavily policed and partitioned societies living in the cities are likely to be the center of crumbling law and order. One prediction tells of killings and looting which follow the earthquake which "hurls Santa Barbara like dice...Soon groups kill to survive". This moment of truth between the "haves" and the "have nots" is settled amidst the tragedy of a nation divided and torn apart.

If the earthquake were to happen in the evening, casualties would be multiplied many times. Millions of people would already be indoors, the rush-hour traffic having cleared. Rescue efforts would be severely hampered by poor light and the true devastation would not be visible until next morning.

Line Three   *Non esloigné du grand eage milliesme*

The solution to this very strange and distorted riddle is located by extraction and anagram.

Non loin du grand age millèsime —
"Not far from the great age-year"

The letters that remain provide the answer.

e	s	g	e	e
5	18	7	5	5
5	9	7	5	5
5 + 9 = 14		(5) + 7 = 21 (3) + 5 = 26 (8) + 5 = 31 (4)		

The bracketted numbers, (5), (3), (8) and (4) make 20 = 2000
The answer to the riddle "not far from the great age-year" is AD 2000.

Finally, the prophecy number again confirms the date, using the standard decoding device of X = 11.

$$X.74 = 11 \; 74 \qquad 7 + 1 = 8 \qquad 4 + 1 = 5$$
$$8th \qquad May$$
$$Year - 1 \quad 1 \quad 7 \quad 4$$
$$7 + 4 + 9 \quad 4 + 7 + 1 + 1 = 13$$
$$9 \qquad 1 \quad 3$$
$$= \quad 193 \quad = \quad 1993$$

All the following predictions extracted from Prophecy X.74 confirm California as the location of the earthquake.

They make grim reading, but it should be obvious that their ultimate aim is not to frighten, but to ALERT and WARN.

"As you enter them, they will come out of their tomb."

A NOTE ON THE DATING

Since the day, month, year, even the hour, of the quake have already been detected, the dating system automatically reflects that change of emphasis, although the techniques employed are the same.

Sections in the time signals may begin or end with 93, or, in many cases, with 5, meaning May. Some sections contain sequences of days – and, where this is vital, "clocks" giving the actual hours and minutes.

Where a series of days appears, the base date, or starting point, will be 8th May, the predicted date of the earthquake.

The Supplementary Dates Section is retained.

Almost ninety years ago in the great earthquake of 1906 troops were called in to stop looting. Law and order are usually the first casualties in countries which have such wide disparities of wealth as there are in the cities of California.

"California clawed up."
7:05 — 8th May 1993

Drawn from verse X.74 Decoded

          b   **p**   **o**
L'Amerique: aprés Roi Charles et Jeux Olympiques, / un
    g   **g**   **m**
grand séisme de San Andreas en California / louve Etat.
    u   **e**   **m l**
Mort tombe en tentes. / Pudeur, danger boiter de zone.

"America: after King Charles and the Olympic Games, a great earthquake from San Andreas in California claws up the State. Death falls among the tents. Decency and danger will limp away from the zone."

Time-Signal

b q	p c	o y	g a	g f	m e	u n	e a	m r	l e
2	15	14	7	7	12	20	5	12	11
16	3	23	1	6	5	13	1	17	5
2	6	5	7	7	3	2	5	3	2
8	3	5	1	6	5	4	1	8	5
2	9	May	8	13	8	6	18	13	10
		8					19	8	May
2:8	=	10	1	+	92	=	93		

BEGINNING IN 1992 and ending in 1993, The coronation of King Charles and the Olympic Games will be followed by a great earthquake, triggered off by a shifting in the San Andreas fault. The earthquake is predicted for 8th May 1993, wreaking huge damage throughout California. Continual tremors and aftershocks will occur after 8th May for at least 13 days.

As a technological and agricultural economy, California outranks most countries in the world. Its leading aerospace and computer industries are situated near the west coast. And, of course, there is Hollywood, the powerhouse of the American film industry which reaps billions of dollars every year from world-wide movie, TV and video sales.

All this is in jeopardy.

The prediction suggests that, following the earthquake, huge camps are set up to accommodate the survivors, but death appears among them during the first six days from 8th May. Possible causes are rioting and disease. Between 8th – 19th May there will be a slow trek, by the more law-abiding citizens, northwards away from the danger zone, including groups of less seriously injured able to walk. Significant dates are 10th, 13th, 18th and 19th.

Still melting down the same verse – X.74 – we can find further information –

"Mass Evacuation." – 1992–1993

<pre>
            p   l   p   m
Evacuation en masse débute des cités et villes avant
                        p   j   n   g
séisme / Rugir le trafic. / Gouverneur de l'Etat organise
            m   m   q   n   u   m
l'exode au bord / ou reste dehors / rond, ombre, zone.
</pre>

"A mass evacuation begins from cities and towns before the earthquake. The traffic will roar. The State Governor organizes the exodus to the border where it stays outside the ring, the shadow, the zone."

Time-Signal

p c	l c	p v	m v	p f	j v	n t	g e	m o	m s	q s	n d	u r	m e
15	11	15	12	15	10	13	7	12	14	16	13	20	12
3	3	21	21	6	21	19	5	14	18	18	4	17	5
6	2	6	3	6	1	4	7	3	5	7	4	2	3
3	3	3	4	6	3	19	5	5	9	9	4	8	5
	92	6 Mar		12			5 July			5 July		8	May
	93	3 Apr			193		May	8	Sept	9		8	May

There is a surrealist atmosphere surrounding this family which calmly dines out complete with tablecloth on salvaged furniture amidst a shattered city in 1906. However, such scenes of peace are unlikely to be common in the next great quake as the incidence of crime has increased beyond all imagination since the turn of this century and Nostradamus clearly sees looting and rioting commonplace as many survivors seek refuge in the North and East.

BETWEEN 6TH MARCH 1992 AND 3 APRIL 1993 there is mass evacuation from Californian towns and cities to other states – apparently a voluntary exercise, with little or no help from the authorities. The sound of traffic driving away will be heard for twelve months, day and night, according to the time-signal dating.

After the earthquake, the State Governor organizes a further exodus of survivors from the state to the border (with Nevada) where they stay. After 5th July this operation ceases, either because there are no more survivors or because those left prefer to try and live where they are.

Between 5th July and 9th September, refugees remain in the camps before, presumably, either traveling back into California or settling elsewhere.

The "ring, shadow, zone" phrase contains the date 8th May twice, which may indicate that there are two major earthquakes as well as a number of severe aftershocks stretching over a period of time.

THE AREA OF THE EARTHQUAKE

The words "ring, shadow, zone" contain map co-ordinates demonstrating that the area of the "ring" is where the greatest seismic disturbance occurs. The "shadow" on the western and northern parameters of the "ring" receive a lesser impact, while the "zone" is that region *outside which* all those hoping to avoid injury or death should remain.

Damage to houses in the 1989 earthquake which Nostradamus foresaw as only a warning of the catastrophy to come.

	N		
ROND			
			13
17	14	13	4
			4
8	5	4	4
			25
	13	17	21

$$17 + 21 = 38$$
$$5 - 2 = 3 \quad 2 - 1 = 1$$

The map co-ordinates are 117–121 degrees longitude by 31–38 degrees latitude.

Note that the calculation includes the date of the earthquake – 8-5 – 8th May.

We can see from the map that the area of greatest seismic disturbance is huge, lying south of the San Andreas fault, extending to the coast, west of Santa Maria and passing directly through the area of San Diego. One the following prediction states that San Diego will disappear beneath the Pacific Ocean. The area stretches southward to points in the Pacific east of Baja California, the peninsula which forms one side of the Gulf of California. A further prediction states that half this territory will be flooded. Enormous geographical changes will occur in this region.

U
OMBRE

		20			
14	13	17	5		
		2			
5	4	8	5		
		24		17 + 22 = 39	4 – 2 = 2
	9	17	22		7 – 1 = 6

The map co-ordinates of the "shadow" area are 117-122 degrees longitude and 26-39 degrees latitude.

This area overlies the "ring" co-ordinates, showing a rim of territory, including San Francisco, where the geographical impact is not so great. Predictions tell of refugees arriving in many thousands in the city.

M
ZONE

			12		
24	14	13	5		
			3		
6	5	4	5		
			23	15 + 20 = 35	3 – 2 = 1
	11	15	20		2 – 0 = 2

The map co-ordinates here are 115-120 degrees longitude and 12-35 degrees latitude.

The "zone" area drawn by Nostradamus is huge, describing the area outside which people should withdraw if they wish to escape injury and death.

The "safety zone" co-ordinates overlap the others given. Therefore, the area of safety *outside which* people should withdraw to the east is 115-117 degrees longitude and 12-35 degrees latitude. The line marking the border of the "safe region" passes close to Las Vegas. Another prediction states that the gambling city becomes a refugee camp after the earthquake.

The safety zone applies to the west coast of the South American continent as far south as 12 degrees latitude which cuts across Nicaragua. Apart from seismic disturbance, this indicates the impact of giant tidal waves originating in the earthquake region. The following predictions support this conclusion.

Nothing comparable to the predicted earthquake in 1993 has yet been experienced in America. Even the worst quake in 1906, shown on the left, is likely to be viewed as a minor event in comparison.

LOGISTIC PROBLEMS

Not only do you have the immediate physical problems of the earthquake, geographical changes, aftershocks, the recovery of the dead and dying, the danger of buildings collapsing, subsidence, flooding – all of which are detailed in following predictions – but these predictions represent a huge social catastrophe. How is it possible to feed hundreds of thousands of people suddenly left without means of support? How is aid got to them if roads and airports are destroyed?

It is clear from these predictions that most of those in the area of the earthquake at the time will have to struggle through to safety themselves if they are to survive.

Therefore, the regions to the north-west, north and east of the earthquake area itself are going to be inundated with refugees.

Continuing the meltdown we move on –

"San Diego Disappears Beneath the Sea."

$$\overset{\text{P}}{\text{San Diego: dur rond. Batiments tomber. Le peuple}}$$

$$\overset{\text{g}}{\text{rotir. L'agonie agrandir. Une masse brune au-dessous la}}$$

$$\overset{\text{m} \qquad \text{z} \quad \text{o} \quad \text{o} \qquad \text{d}}{\text{mer que se jette sur le cit\_ piteux / comme une avalanche.}}$$

*"San Diego: a harsh ring. Buildings fall down. The people will roast.
The agony will increase. A brown mass beneath the sea which rushes
upon the pitiful city like an avalanche."*

Time-Signal

p a	g a	m s	z u	o c	o u	d c
15	7	12	24	14	14	4
1	1	18	20	3	20	3
6	7	3	6	5	5	4
1	1	9	2	3	2	3
	7	93	8 May		5	
7				12	9	7

THE 8TH MAY APPEARS in the center of the time-chart. Left, 7, shows the hour at which the earthquake is predicted to begin. The exact time is 7:05, but the section shows 7:07.

This may indicate that in the first two minutes, buildings fall to the ground and people burn to death, either from fire or electrical accidents.

The city's agony grows. Between 9 and 12 minutes past 7, the Pacific Ocean towers and rushes upon San Diego like an avalanche. Afterwards the city is a brown mass beneath the waters. The geography of this part of the United States will be permanently changed as a result of the earthquake and huge flooding.

The word *Rond* disguises map co-ordinates (see map).

Right: Projected new coastline based upon areas most likely to be flooded. The depth of the saline tidal waters will probably be quite shallow but will render the once fertile land completely useless.

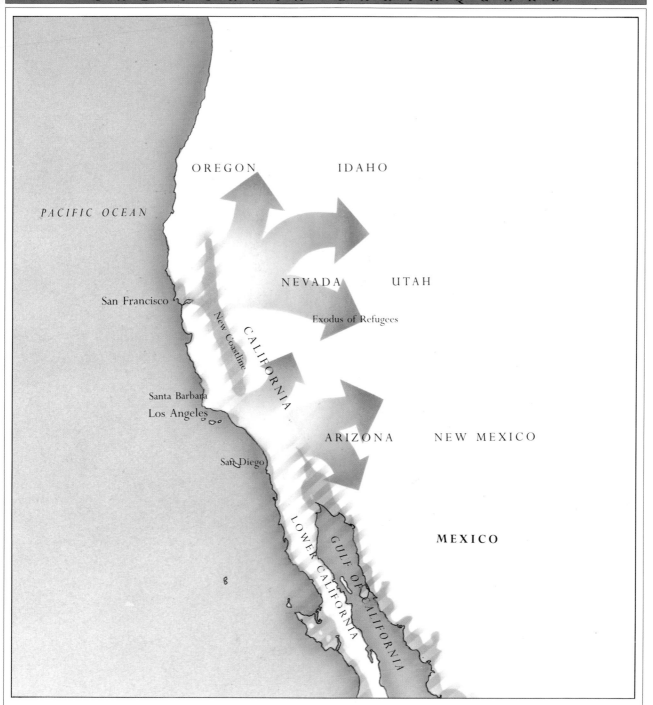

"Giant Waves Hit Mexico."

En demi Baja déluge grand tombe et tonne. Enormes

	p		p		p
h		d	m	l	z	r

vagues / du Golfe de Californie brisent tot sur les rives du

r   **me**

Mexique. Avancent aussi loin que Sonora trempé.

"In half Baja (California) a great deluge falls and thunders. Soon, enormous waves from the Gulf of California break upon the shores of Mexico. They reach as far as steeped Sonora."

Time-Signal

p a	p n	p s	h v	d f	m f	l i	z v	r d	r c	m n	e q
15	15	15	8	4	12	11	24	17	17	12	5
1	13	18	21	6	6	1:9	21	4	3	13	16
6	6	6	8	4	3	2	6	8	8	3	5
1	4	9	3	6	6	19	3	4	3	4	7
				1 (0)							
	12	6	8th		7		8	8	8	11	May
May		9	93	1 + 6 (7)					193	18	14

Any sudden disturbance of the ocean bed can generate tidal waves which can travel at 400 miles per hour and can reach the shore as a series of waves up to 200 feet high.

ONCE AGAIN WE HAVE it confirmed that the earthquake occurs on 8th May 1993. At midnight on the 8th/9th May, five hours after the earthquake has begun, half of Baja California, the tongue of land forming one side of the Gulf of California, is battered by a huge flood from the Pacific, which falls and thunders like cannon fire on the land. Half the land lies under water, perhaps permanently. The fact that the "9th" date is used here, interlinked with 12 o'clock indicates that, as we have already suggested, the earthquake happens at 7:05 p.m. on 8th May, with the flood occurring at midnight. This continues until six.

During the first twelve hours, from seven to seven, "tsunami",

or giant tidal waves, sweep across the Gulf of California towards Mexico's mainland.

The number 8 occurs three times, not only confirming the date, but perhaps also indicating the number of hours before the first wave hits Mexico - 24 - but the worst do not arrive until 11th May (the bigger the wave, the slower it travels).

The waves reach inland as far as the region of Sonora, leaving it steeped or soaked, like marshland. The flood's greatest impact is felt between 11th, 14th and 18th May.

"Los Angeles Undermined."

t   p

Dure ombre. Los Angeles gémir: miné, le cité gronde,

j   a   a

ondule. / Paix. On happe revue dangereuse. / Les morts

a   d   a m   u   z   m

bloquent rue. Constructions / en grandins, nombre ne tient.

"A harsh shadow. Los Angeles will groan. Undermined, the city rumbles and undulates. Peace. A dangerous inspection is snatched. The dead block up the street. Buildings in tiers, a number do not hold."

Time-Signal

t c	p n	j n	a e	a r	a o	d c	a n	m g	u n	z n	m n
19	15	10	1	1	1	4	1	12	20	24	12
3	13	13	5	17	14	3	13	7	13	13	13
19	6	1	1	1	1	4	1	3	2	6	3
3	4	4	5	8	5	3	4	7	4	4	4
		7	10	9	May		5	10	6	10	7
193	8	4	May	8		8			26		

ONCE AGAIN WE SEE that the quake is timed to begin at 7:05. Between 7:04 and 7:08, the city of Los Angeles will actually groan with the stress being put upon its foundations by seismic activity, waves rippling through the ground, which will rumble and undulate.

The word *paix/peace* is a time word.

```
15   1   1:9   22
 6   1   19     4
 6 + 1 = 7     4 + 1 = 5     9 (9 minutes or 9:00)
```

The time, 7:05, is once again evident. The figure "9" indicates either nine minutes after the quake begins, or 9:00 – almost two hours after. This probably defines the length of the quake – nine minutes or 115 minutes. Let us hope that it is the former.

In the great earthquake of 1906 San Francisco suffered a 40 second shockwave followed ten seconds later by another of similar duration. By the time the fires were extinguished three days later the city lay twisted, broken and scorched by fire. Now it is believed that the death toll was over 3000; over 500 city blocks were destroyed and 300,000 people were made homeless. The shock waves prophesied by Nostradamus may last

an hour and a half so the destruction and number of deaths could be far more terrible than that of 1906.

Above: Fighting fires in the San Francisco earthquake of 1989.

The 9th and 10th May see a dangerous inspection after the quake, probably to search for victims and survivors, and from the onset of the disaster, the streets and buildings will be blocked by the dead.

Buildings are sheered away, their floors resembling the tiers of theaters. Many, of course, fall to the ground. The number "26" seems significant. This may be either the full length of time it takes to destroy Los Angeles, or a record of the number of major buildings destroyed during the quake's effect on the city.

Dure ombre/harsh shadow is a geographical reference to the extent of the quake (See map)

"Hollywood Film Studios Collapse."

buu   m   j   v   d   x

Hollywood goguenard anerie tragique. Sera / à la traine les

u   g   m   m   z   d

autres en préparations pour / le séisme. Le sol tombe. Les / studios

e   t m   b

s'écroulent, pas un seul indemné.

"Mocking Hollywood — a tragic stupidity. It will lag behind the others in preparations for the earthquake. The ground subsides. The studios collapse, not one undamaged."

Time-Signal

b y	m u	j a	v s	d a	x l	u s	g u	m s	m l	z l	d s	e o	t s	m u	b l
2	12	10	21	4	22	20	7	12	12	24	4	5	19	12	2
23	20	1	18	1	11	18	20	18	11	11	18	14	18	20	11
2	3	1	3	4	4	2	7	3	3	6	4	5	19	3	2
5	2	1	9	1	2	9	2	9	2	2	9	5	9	2	2
Feb	4		93	Aug		9		93	May	8	33	May		193	?
5th	Mar			1	Feb		92				29	20	15	6	4

WITH YEARS OF EXPERIENCE at making fantasy disaster movies – including the finest details and realistic setting – Hollywood pays little or no attention when the real thing is about to arrive!

Between the 4th February and 5th March 1993, Hollywood ridicules the notion of the predicted earthquake, perhaps fearing but not believing the predicted destruction of the film industry, the biggest reason for the town's existence.

From 9th August 1992, it lags behind other towns and cities in making preparations.

Again, for the umpteenth time, we see 8th May as the date of the commencement of the quake. Within 33 minutes of the quake beginning, all the buildings and studio lots collapse.

"San Francisco – Refugees Flee Devastation"

u x   d   b   d
Je nomme Saint Francois que retentira de bruit éloigné
g   m   m   e
du sol paralléle séisme. / Puits, pompes gondolent. Après
z   o   d   u   b
un veille, refugiés arrivent tot à marcher.

"I name 'Saint Francis' which reverberates with distant sound from the ground parallel to the earthquake. Shafts, pumps buckle. After a night watch, refugees soon arrive on foot."

Time-Signal

u	x	d	b	d	g	m	m	e	z	o	d	u	b
a	f	i	i	i	r	s	l	p	l	f	v	t	c
20	22	4	2	4	7	12	12	5	24	14	4	20	2
1	6	1:9	1:9	1:9	17	18	11	15	11	6	21	19	3
2	4	4	2	4	7	3	3	5	6	5	4	2	2
1	6	19	19	19	8	9	2	6	2	6	3	19	3
16	14	10	6	4	7	93	14*	11		May 8			
17	23	42	8	20	8	28	16*	22	24	30	33	19	3

9 May 11 hours after 7:05 6:00 a.m. 24 May 11 hours after 7:00 p.m.
14 "   "   "   9:00   10 May 30 "   "   1:00 a.m.
16 "   "   "   11:00   33 "   "   4:00 a.m.
22 "   "   "   5:00 p.m.

* The numbers 14 and 16 can be reduced to 5 and 7, or 7:05, the time of the earthquake, an added confirmation to the date in this section.

This prediction contains an amazing amount of information, including a prime device which confirms, once and for all, the rule of the "Substitute Letter" (one substitute letter per word).

The name "San Francisco" has been changed to the French equivalent – *Saint Francois*. Nostradamus confirms this in the most extraordinary way – he states that he himself NAMES the city in this prediction, lest anyone should think this is an arbitrary decision on the part of the interpreter!

The financial district of San Fransisco. The disruption of the entire banking and finance system of the west coast has far reaching consequences for the entire federation and especially for an economy already in recession. The United States will lick its economic wounds long after the turn of the century and its status as a super power could crumble in much the same manner as that of the U.S.S.R. in 1990.

The left-hand part of the time-signal counts the number of minutes during which people in San Francisco hear the terrible sound of the earthquake reverberating through the ground beneath their feet. It begins one minute before the earthquake, at 7:04 and continues until at least 8:28 – a period of one hour and twenty-four minutes. Most earthquakes last only a few minutes, excluding aftershocks.

The period 7:42 – 8:20 is produced from the number 19 on three occasions, suggesting that the loudest reverberations occur then. Sound waves take longer to travel through rock than through air and the sound during this period would be coming from the southern part of the State where the destruction is worst.

In San Francisco itself, "shafts and pumps buckle", referring to mineshafts and other underground shafts, water and sewage systems, wells, gas stations and any other facility which uses pumping equipment.

The right time-signal again seems to confirm that the earthquake occurs at 7:05 p.m. on the evening of 8th May 1993.

Nostradamus says that it is after a "night watch" that refugees from the earthquake region begin to arrive. This makes sense. If the earthquake occurred at 7:05 a.m. people fleeing from the area would not take eleven hours of sunlight to begin arriving. They would appear within an hour or two. But amidst such devastation and at night, they would have to stay put until daybreak.

However, by 10th May they are arriving at night with perhaps a lighting system set up to guide them (San Francisco could have lost its electricity supply at first), together with, perhaps, the first rescue attempts to bring groups of refugees out.

Refugees arrive on foot – no roads are passable for vehicles within the earthquake region itself to the northwest of the state.

"California after the Earthquake."
1993-1995

Drawn from verse III.65

l   p   e j

Amerique, non sagesse,/recouvre du séisme – prédit,/su, vu en o

o   s   n a   uu n d

California; San Francisco /pont rasé / reconstruit; Hollywood haut/

a   g   a

repeuplé. Guerre en Europe

"America unwisely recovers from the predicted, known and seen earthquake in California; the destroyed San Francisco bridge rebuilt; the heights of Hollywood repopulated. War in Europe."

Time-Signal

l	p	e	j	o	s	n	s	a	n	d	a	g	a
i	r	i	u	f	c	t	a	c	o	t	e	r	o
11	15	5	10	14	18	13	18	1	13	4	1	7	1
1:9	17	1:9	20	6	3	19	1	3	14	19	5	17	14
2	6	5	1	5	9	4	9	1	4	4	1	7	1
19	8	19	2	6	3	19	1	3	5	19	5	8	5
	6	195	1	95			94	Jan	4	194			9
192	Aug			Aug		19	Jan	3	May		May	8	5
			Mar		93								
				6									

NB – uu is only a split form of w and does not form a true substitute or have any numerical value.

NOSTRADAMUS, IN OTHER PREDICTIONS indicates that the California earthquake of 1993 will surpass all others hitherto experienced in magnitude. In ferocity it will exceed Krakatoa (1888). In his verse X.74 he states that the prospect is not all darkness, however, and that lives will be saved because the prediction of the quake is known before it happens and a mass evacuation of the region will take place.

In the prediction on the previous page, the prophet insists once again that a sequence of events, not at all characteristic of this cynical age, will help the situation – prediction followed by belief in prediction, followed by action based on this belief and finally the quake itself. Normally, our response in the past has simply been disbelief followed by inaction followed by the event, by which time everyone has forgotten that there was a prediction in the first place and those that have not put it down to coincidence!

The problem is that the human mind is so conditioned to disbelieve in the process of prediction, or anything else unexplained, that it has an automatic "cut-out" process which denies the truth. Even as these words are being read, many people will simply shrug their shoulders and cast the ideas contained herein aside as crankish nonsense. It may be, however, that in 1993 the California earthquake will help re-establish the powers of prediction again. California is, after all, one of the most forward-looking areas of the world when it comes to esoteric concepts.

Geographical references for this massive quake are clearly defined – America, California, San Francisco, Hollywood, Europe. Nostradamus wishes us to be in no doubt about the point he is making. The *whole* of America will recover from the quake, not simply one state. America is *looking back* on the quake, predicted for 8th May 1993. All of California awaits this disturbance of the earth.

The time-signal indicates, in the left-hand column, that in 1992 "America unwisely recovers....", this being *before* the quake has occurred in terms of chronology! But Nostradamus often played this game with his prophecies. If we can visualize the bizarre nature of his verses, spread across time as though it were a tapestry, past, present and future all laid out before him. We, as characters stitched into this tapestry, are now observing the situation in *his* future, but with the event still in *our* future! The predicted event, however, discusses the quake as though it were in the past! The whole thing becomes very hard to be sensible about! The line in this case is split into time frames – the first three words in 1992, but referring to an event in 1993 about which America unwisely acted, perhaps because not sufficient concern was given to the prophet's warning before the quake, which then resulted in worse losses of life – a consideration of regret *after the quake*. Perhaps we can see by this stream of time and space just how extraordinarily difficult it must have been to construct the verses in the first place – let alone the complexity of the codes to hide the truth from the intermediate generations.

Bridges are often the earliest casualties in earthquakes so are built stronger in regions of seismic disturbance. In the 1989 earthquake a section was damaged on the Oakland Bay bridge but was repaired in a relatively short time.

Looking again at the time-signal – by 6th August 1995 America is already recovering from the quake. During the time span between 6th March 1993 and 1st August 1995 there is intense public interest in the earthquake in San Francisco. The quake happens on May 8th 1993 and the Golden Gate Bridge is severely damaged so that perhaps the remaining parts still standing are pulled down and rebuilding commences after 19th January 1994.

Between 4th January and 3rd May 1994 the "heights of Hollywood" begin to be repopulated – a casual statement which suggests that the area must have been severely affected by the quake. The suggestion is clear and creates a strange picture of the most famous fantasy factory in the world being empty and like a ghost town for a considerable period of time.

The verse suggests indirectly that the worst part of the quake damage is suffered in the east and south of the area, not in the north.

The last line switches dramatically to Europe and if we examine the time-signal once again we see that there is war there two years after the quake has taken place.

NORTH AMERICA – AFTER THE QUAKE

"America Burns" - 1993 - 1996

Drawn from verse III.65

    o   p   j   p
Aprés le séisme, les Etats-Unis/fusant dans un rayon qu'étend de t rive à
               t   p   p   n   g
  rive./ On rougir. Sous chaud soleil,/ la récolte en feu, troupeaux
    s   c   h
meurent./ Grain rare.

"After the earthquake, the United States is crackling within a radius which stretches from coast to coast. Everything will redden. Under a hot sun, crops are on fire, flocks and herds die. Grain is scarce."

Time-Signal

ɔ	p	j	p	t	p	p	n	g	s	c	h
l	t	t	t	r	i	t	f	x	t	i	a
14	15	10	15	19	15	15	13	7	18	3	8
11	19	19	19	17	1:9	19	6	22	19	1:9	1
5	6	1	6	19	6	6	4	7	9	3	8
2	19	19	19	8	19	19	6	4	19	19	1
5	196	191	196	198	196	196	4	7	199	193	8
Feb						June	Apr			Jan	
										Mar 8	191

Even in the late 1980's a drought threatened Californian farmlands. This will intensify during the next five years until the once rich and fertile region becomes hardly more than desert.

AFTER THE CALIFORNIA EARTHQUAKE of 1993 detailed in the last pages, the statement that United States "is crackling" indicates that a major burning of the earth, presumably crop failure and drought, continues over a period. "Everything is reddened" — land and people are flushed with the heat, probably suffering from the effects of too much heat and the exhaustion of dehydration. Nostradamus is viewing an America as if it were a time/space map with "redness" as the general picture he wished to convey.

The devastation of American agriculture by climatic change develops out of global warming over a period of years, but there is particular emphasis on the 5th February 1996. Uncontrollable brush and forest fires will begin again in 1991, as they have already done so in 1990 with the California and Arkansas fires. Over the years to 1996, this problem increases until almost every state experiences it. Between 1996-8 almost everywhere reddens in the heat, indicating widespread problems with many deaths.

Grain is scarce over the period from 8th March 1991 to 8th January 1993, perhaps because of vital supplies being stored in order to overcome fears of future scarcity. We may even see similar scenes as are presently being experienced in Moscow, with queues for food in the streets, or rationing of food. This would be a first for America.

Forest fires like the one opposite at Yellowstone, devastated one and a half million acres in the Western states in 1988 after a long drought. *Above:* An army helicopter flies towards the fire for a water drop. When pitted against raging fires such as these even the most sophisticated technology seems pitiful.

"Spacecraft crashes on America" – 1997

Drawn from verse III.65

    g   o   o   n   j

Un vaisseau / spatial Russien choir sur l'Amerique. / Deux personnes morts.

      s   p   o   a

Le Chef Yeltsin ne fera guére entendre / l'acrimonie. Dupe prouvé au sang

 s

perdu.

"A Russian spacecraft will crash on America. Two people killed. The leader Yeltsin will hardly listen to the acrimony. A fool shown up by bloodshed."

Time-Signal

g i	o i	o i	n r	j x	s z	p f	o t	a m	s e
7	14	14	13	10	18	15	14	1	18
1:9	1:9	1:9	17	22	24	6	19	12	5
7	4	4	4	1	9	6	5	1	9
19	19	19	8	4	6	6	19	3	5
			4	Jan		6	195	Jan	5
197	194	194	Aug	4	96	June		3	95

It would seem from this prediction that Boris Yeltsin (above) has managed to oust President Gorbachev (inset) from power. It may, however, suggest that the Republic of Russia is running a space program independently from the Federation of Soviet states.

I N THIS PREDICTION we see the first part of the time-signal dating the most important aspect of the story – 1997. This is the year, as we will see in the "Science and Technology" predictions, when physics opens up new areas of scientific discovery that will influence space travel. Everything else that comes, time-wise, thereafter in this prediction is in reference to that discovery.

The prediction also links up with another which we will find later in the book (Britain in Europe) in which a crashing spacecraft is mentioned. The craft in the prediction on this page appears to crash on 4th August 1994. If Boris Yeltsin is still President of Russia then, this indicates that the Republic of Russia is running its own space

program independent of whatever remains of the Soviet Union. The fact that he does not listen to objections indicates that the space program will continue to be pursued but will run into other difficulties between 6th June 1995 and 4th January 1996.

On 3rd January 1995 there is to be a bitter argument between the US and Russia. Nostradamus seems not to be impressed by the leader's response.

WORLD FIGURES

"Margaret Thatcher — Conservative Leader Again." — 1996

Quand le pont / plonger, sionisme sévir. Aurore lueur prés feux. / Paul —

(n s u u n above)

gué à Dieu. Margaret Thatcher /remonte à devenir chef des / Conservateurs

(p d o j s p above)

— sans loins.

(y above)

"When the bridge will submerge, zionism will rage. Dawn, a glimmer beside the fires. Paul — a ford to God. Margaret Thatcher remounts to become leader of the Conservatives — without the reins."

Time-Signal

n	s	u	u	n	p	d	o	j	s	p	y
t	r	m	r	x	t	h	t	f	d	v	i
13	18	20	20	13	15	4	14	10	18	15	23
19	17	12	17	22	19	8	19	6	4	21	1:9
4	9	2	2	4	6	4	5	1	9	6	5
19	8	3	8	4	19	8	19	6	4	3	19
194		92	2	Apr	196	4	195	1	Sept	6	195
						Aug		Oct		Mar	
	98	3	Dec					196	4		

Thatcher as seen by the British newspaper, the Evening Standard. The image of the ex-prime minister of the U.K. in the role of Marlene Dietrich in "Blue Angel" is particularly effective as Margaret Thatcher has never hidden her distrust of Germany. Her general anti-European stance was just one of the issues which cost her the leadership of the country in 1990.

AMERICA WILL BE MUCH INVOLVED in the problems of the after effects of her own home tragedy, the California earthquake — the Golden Gate Bridge, for example will have been so seriously damaged that the remnants of it will be pulled down and the whole thing rebuilt. As we have seen in earlier quake predictions, places like Hollywood will literally no longer exist. There

will be little space for serious foreign affairs interest so that her relationship with Israel will be neglected. During the years between 2nd April 1992 and 3rd December 1998 the zionist movement will dominate the political scene creating great turmoil and conflict. Pope John Paul II will pass away.

"Dawn, a glimmer beside the fires" – fires presumably raging across the United States, ruining crops, animals and causing human and economic devastation. This "dawn" – rising in the east – may also have some relevance to Middle Eastern conflict with Israel (see Middle East predictions).

"Paul – a ford to God…" This is a reference to John Paul II's prophetic and historical significance. His election to office in 1978 was the catalyst for the first political movement in the Polish shipyards at Gdansk which led to the rise of the *Solidarity* movement. His reign has thus seen the fall of communism in Europe and its gradual retreat in the Soviet Union. It has been the "ford" by which the nations of Europe will cross to unity, and at his passing, he will go to God with this aspect of the world's changes best remembered. It is, moreover, the divine reason why his tragic predecessor, John Paul I, died so early.

Karol Wojtyla, John Paul II, had been destined from birth to oversee these momentous events in Europe, which will alter the course of the world for centuries to come. The destiny was shown in other predictions long before its occurrence and this may be seen, in the light of Nostradamus' predictions, as the reason for the quick change in papal office.

This remarkable prediction emerged during the summer of 1990, months before the political earthquake which led to Margaret Thatcher's resignation on 22nd November 1990. According to Nostradamus, the story of Margaret Thatcher as a political phenomenon is not yet over.

She rises to prominence once more on 4th August 1996. Between 1st September 1995 and 4th October 1996, she appears to be climbing back to power as leader of the Conservatives, perhaps even becoming Prime Minister of Great Britain again. The date 6th March 1995 may be the time of her re-election to leadership of the party. However, there is the hint that she may only become leader of the opposition, as perhaps the Conservatives are no longer in power.

A tearful and not so "Iron Lady" leaves No. 10 Downing Street for what appeared to be the last time.

"Mitterrand Government Accused."
1994–1998

Drawn from verse I.42

    e   x   d   d

France: Scandale politique. Michel Noir cite /

         a   e   i   d

le feu gouvernement du Mitterrand concernant / largesses,

    d   t   i

corruptions. Blessé a l'assaillant / Hébraique.

"*France: political scandal. Michel Noir cites the late government of Mitterrand concerning gifts and corruptions. Wounded by a Hebrew assailant.*"

Time-Signal

e a	x n	d o	d t	a r	e r	i n	d r	d o	t n	i r
5	22	4	4	1	5	1:9	4	4	19	1:9
1	13	14	19	17	17	13	17	14	13	17
5	4	4	4	1	5	19	4	4	19	19
1	4	5	19	8	8	4	8	5	4	8
May	8		194	1	May		4	Apr		
	5	May		Aug	8	194	Aug	5	194	198

I N DECEMBER 1990 MICHEL NOIR, mayor of Lyon and a leading member of the French right-wing party RPR, resigned from both the party and his parliamentary seat, an action viewed as a long-term step towards his standing in the next French presidential election in 1995.

During the period 5th to 8th May 1994 Noir accuses the Mitterrand government of corruption. The scandal arises from 1st May (when he possibly makes his decision to speak out) to 8th August.

He may obtain evidence of such corruption during 4th April and 5th August.

Above: Michel Noir, right wing mayor of Lyon.

Although the number 198 would normally mean 1998, here it is possibly 19th August, the date of the attempted assassination mentioned in the prediction.

It does not say whether he recovers, or whether he goes on to become President of France in 1995.

Above: Francois Mitterand at a press conference during the Gulf crisis.

"Richard Gere Abandons Hollywood." – 1993

Drawn from verse I.42

    x   **q b**

Aprés la nuit longue du séisme, l'acteur / Richard Gere

 q   **d**

ne revient pas au cité couchant des films. / Foi se

   t   **n**

coalise avec le Dalai Lama sage de Tibet en l'Inde.

"*After the long night of the earthquake, the actor Richard Gere does not return to the sleeping city of films. His faith joins forces with the wise Dalai Lama of Tibet in India.*"

Time-Signal

x	q	b	q	d	t	n
a	e	a	r	a	v	g
22	16	2	16	4	19	13
1	5	1	17	1	21	7
4	7	2	7	4	19	4
1	5	1	8	1	3	7
4	9			July 4		Apr
1		June		9	193	7

Richard Gere with his wife, the former Cindy Crawford.

FILM STAR RICHARD GERE, practising Buddhist and spokesman in the West for the plight of China-occupied Tibet, will not return to Hollywood.

The 'long night' of the earthquake during which the 'sleeping city of films' is either deserted or inactive will last from 8th May 1993 – the predicted date of the quake – until 1st June 1994, when attempts to revive the industry could be made.

In July, perhaps following a grim public assessment of Hollywood's prospects of renewal, Gere will make the decision not to go back.

The prediction appears to indicate that from 7th April 1993, a month before the earthquake, Gere will have been staying with the

The actor seen with the exiled Dalai Lama of Tibet.

Dalai Lama in India where the respected religious leader fled after the Chinese invasion of his country in 1959.

The prediction does not suggest that Gere will give up making films, nor does it mention his new wife, Cindy Crawford.

"President Nelson Mandela." – 1994

Drawn from verse 1.35

    j   **y**   **x**
L'Afrique du sud – Le President Nelson Mandela lui-même, un moribond,
    y x v   **y** **u** **r**
gère le role / des voix noires/ pullullants. Séche chaleur / croft. Un virus
    u
caserné cueille page.

"*South Africa: President Nelson Mandela himself, a dying man, manages the register of multiplying black voices. The dry heat grows. A quartered virus plucks a page of history.*"

Time-Signal

j	y	x	y	x	v	y	u	u	r	u
f	n	d	d	o	o	s	h	t	n	n
10	23	22	23	22	21	23	20	20	17	20
6	13	4	4	14	14	18	8	19	13	13
1	5	4	5	4	3	5	2	2	8	2
6	4	4	4	5	5	9	8	19	4	4
July		9		9	3	5	2	192		10
	4	4	Apr	10		9	Aug	Aug.		

Above: Nelson Mandela and his wife Winnie, who during 1991, appeared in court charged with kidnapping and assault. By 1994 both seem to have survived a case which may have proved too embarrassing for a government to press, engaged as it was in a policy of reconciliation with a black community headed by Mandela himself.

IN SOUTH AFRICA, Nelson Mandela is President on 4th July 1994. Though a dying man, he has overseen the huge task of vote registration and electoral reform for the black South Africans (10th April 1993). The country is, like others, severely affected by climatic change. A hot drought is spreading (2nd August 1995). Meanwhile, a virus, possibly AIDS, has been quartered in the country since 10th August 1992. Its arrival marks the end of a page of history.

"Fonda and Turner before the Senate."
– 19th April 1993

Drawn from verse III.65

>   **h**   **g**   **l**
> *Mai, un pis-aller. Jane Fonda, Ted Turner vus prédiction publié du seisme*
>   **n**   **g**   **a**   **p**   **h**
> *roule / pont cassé, / voyageront au Senat que les ouir, / or se leurre sans*
>   **e**
> *un respect.*

"May, a last resort. Jane Fonda, Ted Turner having seen the prediction of the rolling earthquake, the broken bridge, will travel to the Senate, which will hear them, but deceives itself without reason."

Time-Signal

Mai is a time word – 12 1 1:9 = 3   1 19
                              = 19 4
                              = 19th April 1993.

h	g	l	n	g	a	p	h	e
l	b	i	t	t	t	i	l	t
8	7	11	13	7	1	15	8	5
11	2	19	19	19	19	1:9	11	19
8	7	2	4	7	2	6	8	5
2	2	19	19	19	19	19	2	19
Aug	7	192	194	197	192	196	8	195
2	Feb						Feb	

The time word *Mai* gives the date of this last desperate appeal by two famous names as 19th April 1993. The earthquake is predicted for 8th May and it is clear that this prediction describes events immediately before it occurs.

Previous page and right: Jane Fonda and Ted Turner. It is likely that the actress-activist might well voice a strong belief in the prophecies of Nostradamus. It would also be logical that Ted Turner, as chairman of cable News Network might give backing to any renewed interest in the prophet.

Jane Fonda and Ted Turner, at time of writing, are due to be married. Some while before the earthquake is due to occur they will become convinced of the validity of the predictions and will travel to the Senate in Washington to appear and make an appeal for evacuation of the area and special aid for the damage expected. Although the Senate will listen to their appeal it will be too much to expect formal government to take a serious interest in something so apparently "vague" as a four-hundred year old prophecy in this scientific age. They will not give this as their reason for non-action, however.

The time-signal dates indicate that Fonda and Turner will become increasingly concerned between 2nd February and either 7th August 1992 or 1993 (this is not entirely clear). The Golden Gate Bridge also appears once again here but the information is not quite clear either, insofar as this interpretation indicates that the bridge remains collapsed after the quake until 1994 whereas other verses indicate that it will be pulled down for rebuilding.

In 1992 and 1996/7, Fonda and Turner will become further involved in the quake's results – debates and discussions with the political legislature – and from 8th February 1995 it will be made clear that the Senate will refuse to take action based on the approaches of these two well-known personalities.

SCIENCE AND TECHNOLOGY

"Advanced Technology Saves the German Economy." 1995 – 2000

Drawn from verse X.22

  r   p   r   r   r p

Sine die, l'économie d'Allemagne assigne un risque au

      r r   u   q u   i r

puvoir. Science et technologies avancées y s'associent en

    i u   r   i

produisant les issues. foudroyantes.

"The German economy places an indefinite risk on the government. Here, science and advanced technologies join together in producing stunning solutions."

Time-Signal

r	p	r	r	r	p	r	r	u	q	u	i	r	i	u	r	i
e	c	m	n	n	e	e	t	n	s	s	t	e	t	l	s	t
17	15	17	17	17	15	17	17	20	16	20	1:9	17	1:9	20	17	1:9
5	3	12	13	13	5	6	19	13	18	18	19	5	19	11	18	19
8	6	8	8	8	6	8	8	2	7	2	19	8	19	2	8	19/10
5	3	3	4	4	5	5	19	4	9	9	19	5	19	2	9	19/10
Aug 5	Aug 9	Aug 3	Aug 4	Aug 4	6 Aug 10		198 Apr	2	92/7/9			198 195		192	98	2000

*Coding: 10 = 2000

A SIMPLE PREDICTION WITH COMPLEX dating — Nostradamus, aware of Germany's economic power in this decade, has separated the stages in this process.

Already, pressures on the German economy are growing, following unification. The Latin phrase *sine die*/indefinitely may indicate friction with partners in the Treaty of Rome over Germany's heavy financial burden in the European community.

A low point in her economy will be reached during 3rd — 4th August 1995, resulting in unstable government — already, right-wing extremist groups are gaining influence in elections. Connected problems will occur until after 6th August 2000.

However, between 1995 — 1998 scientific advances will give rise to powerful new technologies which eventually transform the German economy and other economies within Europe. These technologies will become prominent between 1997 — 1999, taking on a new momentum after 2nd April 1998. They will provide answers to many economic difficulties, resulting in the easing of political pressures.

The entire process may be triggered off by a scientific discovery in 1992, its practical value perhaps not being appreciated for several years.

Between 1998 — 2000, there is a huge acceleration in these revolutionary technological solutions — they will eliminate waste in many areas and go on to establish much simpler, more efficient ways of producing and providing within society.

Throughout this book, Nostradamus strongly predicts the beginning of a new scientific age after 1995.

The headquarters of the Deutsche Bank in Frankfurt. This city is the nerve centre of Europe's banking system and the once booming economy of the 1980s is reflected in the optimism of the high rise office buildings — the tallest in Europe.

"*Siécles* * Alters the Human Brain." – 1999

Drawn from verse I.42

             g t   **f**   **b**

La fiche prophétique Siécles alignera les cerveaux / humains des gens qui

    l   **t**   **e**   **t**   **t**   **i**

désirent le science de Nostradamus. / Ont du bol, à cause / d'amas dans

    i

   linceuls.

"*The prophetic timetable Siécles will align the human brains of people who want the science of Nostradamus. They are fortunate, because of the mass of ideas within the shrouds.*"

Time-Signal

g a	t s	f h	b g	l n	t s	e u	t u	t s	i s	i s
7	19	6	2	11	19	5	19	19	1:9	1:9
1	18	8	7	13	18	20	20	18	18	18
7	19	6	2	2	19	5	19	19	19	19
1	9	8	7	4	9	2	2	9	9	9
1999	-	8	Feb	1999		May	92	1999	1999	1999
1	July		August	11		2nd				

**Siécles* is the French title of Nostradamus' work of prediction - The Centuries.*

NOSTRADAMUS STATES CLEARLY in this prediction that the continued use of predictive devices such as the study of his own verses, can eventually result in a personal power to predict on the part of the student. The "shrouds" describe the distorted quatrains of the Siecles.

By the 1st July 1999, just before the end of the millennium, the power of prophecy has become an established ability acceptable to mankind. This appears to begin its process from 2nd February 1992, perhaps as a result of this book.

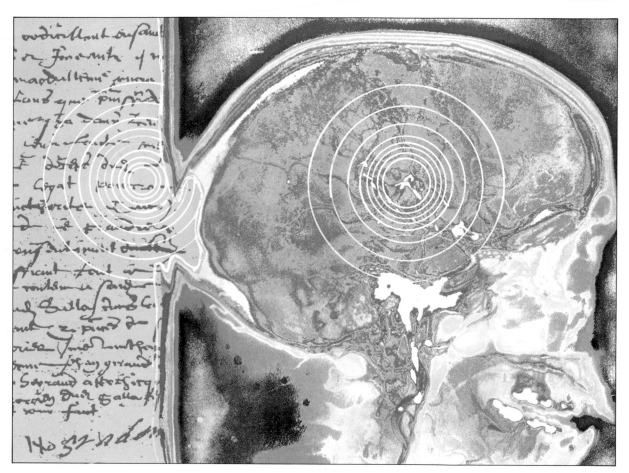

It is recognised that our perceptions are largely formed by what we expect to perceive. Nostradamus cuts through our habitual view of the material world and the idea that the future is not really accessible to us. The prophet clearly shows that it can be seen by those attuned to it.

It is important to note the emphasis on a change of brain usage, or brain pattern – a change that is needed to accept and use prediction as a real force in life. One of the major reasons why this has not been possible during this century until now is the presence of "rational" science and its determination, also backed by the established Church, not to accept anything that does not emanate from the thinking or reasonable capacities of the brain. This is becoming so patently absurd as a dictum that the human brain is opening up to the unreasonable at last, and finding it continuously fascinating. The presence of the "unreasonable" chaos theories illustrates this. If chaos can be converted from unreasonable to reasonable simply by understanding, so also can prediction.

"Computers Calculate Chaos." — 1996

Drawn from verse I.35

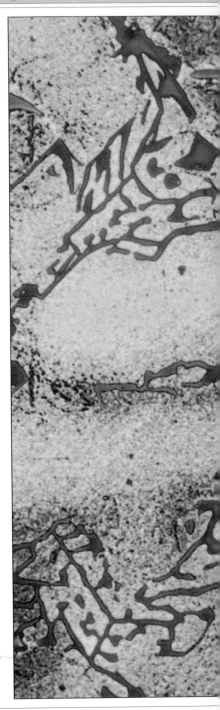

           y   **p**   **y**

Dix ordinateurs jumellent, liquide a gueule, morcellent/ calculer sans lier les

   y   **a**

les unités. Révéle du chaos, un rêve nouveau, simple. Gère loix mûrir les

    x

cubes purs.

"*Ten computers are paired off, liquid to the mouth. They break into pieces to calculate without binding the units. Revealed by chaos, a new and simple dream. It manages laws to mature pure cubes.*"

Time-Signal

y l	p t	y s	y t	a s	x e
23	15	23	23	1	22
11	19	18	19	18	5
5	6	5	5	1	4
2	19	9	19	9	5
5	196	5	195	91	9
Feb		Sept			=2000

THE FOCUS OF THIS PREDICTION IS CHAOS, referring to the theory which first rose to prominence in the 1970s. Scientists have chosen the subject as their most recent and popular fashion, making chaos the center of widespread theoretical experimentation.

Readers will not perhaps readily appreciate the nature of chaos as its modern application has developed. To give a simple example – scientists involved in chaos theory use the half-serious example of the flapping of a butterfly's wings. This might seem a totally random affair with little or no likely effect on the surroundings – so to speak, a random and ineffective movement. But modern science has actually linked what it calls "sensitive dependence on initial

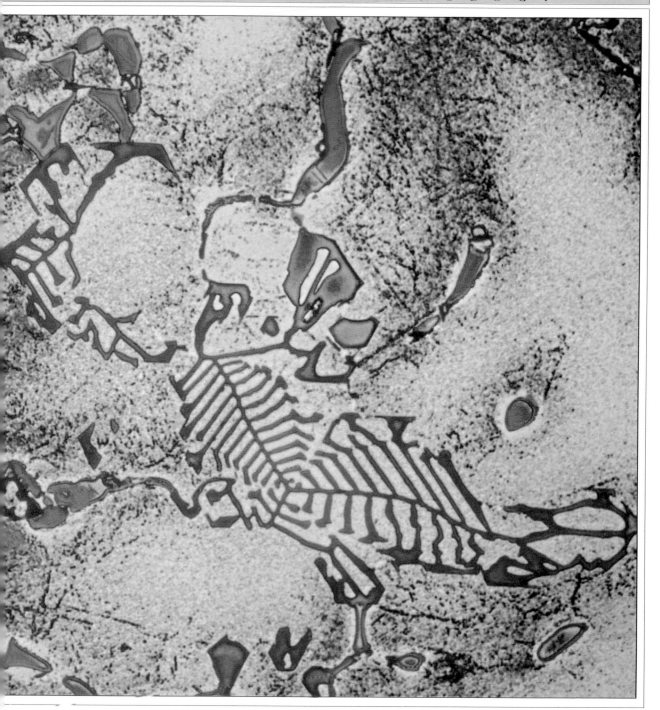

conditions" to traceable results - the movement of butterfly wings, say in the Pacific Ocean, to the upsurge of a hurricane! The concept, actually exemplified, indicates that even the tiniest movement or change of physical activity anywhere on the planet touches the rest of the planet – even though the change that occurs may be of infinitesimal value – it still theoretically has an effect.

Chaos theory therefore explains that in a sense chaos is only something which we don't necessarily understand. Chaos in this context is therefore irrelevant and anything which we consider chaotic may in fact be perfectly sensible.

Chaos theory is now a highly developed factor of mathematics and is being applied to all manner of hitherto unfathomable aspects of science and matter. The ecosystem of this planet is, of course, a prime target for chaos theory.

The prediction on this page might easily seem a perfect example of chaos theory. The arrangement of the melted-down words was one of the most difficult to figure out and this factor has two effects – firstly that it indicates the nature of the prediction, but secondly it also gives way to other possible interpretations. The problem is that much of the scientific theory involved, although it may have been clear to the prophet Nostradamus, is not apparent to us. It has not happened yet and we do not have much to go on!

Essentially we are being told about a computer system that has not been developed but appears to have something to do with five pairs of computers working together. "Liquid to the mouth" suggests that one of the pairs feeds the other with information – perhaps some kind of random system to illustrate the senses of chaos in any given situation. These streams of information may change their form or nature when transmitted to one another.

The computers start their work on 5th February 1996 following a simple new theory proposed on 5th September 1995. The use of the word "dream" indicates a right brain source. Nostradamus uses this analogy frequently.

Very large computer capacity is required to prove the theory which proposes the new laws of chaos and the final date is 2000 when mathematical models involving pure cubes will be produced. Using such models perhaps we will be able to predict ecosystems and other complex systems enabling mankind to reverse the ecological damage that has occurred.

Previous page: "Chinese Script" is an apt name for the complex dendrites of various trace metals found in this aluminium-silicon alloy. Existence creates such seemingly chaotic patterns which the human mind promptly seeks to give some sense of order. Perhaps chaos is merely a concept which reflects that particular obsession.

Right: The Cray machine, at the US National Supercomputing Center at the University of Illinois, uses "parallel processing" which allows information to be processed in a way analogous to that which occurs within the human brain. Such computers can be seen as the parents of the forthcoming generations of super machines which promises to be radically more intelligent than their ancestors.

"Mission to Mars." – 2000

Drawn from verse X.22

      i   i   i r   r

Mars connu. Voyage à la planéte / près le Grand Age. Puissance nouvelle

   i   i   i   r   s   i   r

que / croît / au lieu de diminuer. Un succés / foudroyant. Possession

       s   i

hors de roquette.

"Mars known. A journey to the planet near to the great age. A new power which grows instead of lessens. A staggering success. Possession outside the rocket."

Time-Signal

i	i	i	r	r	i	i	i	r	s	i	r	s	i
a	t	e	u	l	e	t	l	m	u	t	n	d	t
1:9	1:9	1:9	17	17	1:9	1:9	1:9	17	18	1:9	17	18	1:9
1	19	5	20	11	5	19	11	12	20	19	13	4	19
19	19	19	8	8	19	19	19	8	9	19	8	9	19
1	19	5	2	2	5	19	2	3	2	19	4	4	19
191		198		Aug		2000	198			2000	Aug	Sep	2000
2000		May	2	2	195		Feb	3	92		4	4	

19/19 refers to the year 2000. 19+19 = 38 = 11 = 2 = 2000

MARS, OUR CLOSEST PLANETARY NEIGHBOR after the Moon, is visited for the first time by humans during a space voyage which ends in a landing on the red planet in 2000, perhaps a breathtaking piece of millennium – ending drama. The planning for this begins in 1991.

A new technology is mentioned in the verse, heralded by the statement that it "grows instead of lessens." The new method of travel will not make use of the massively heavy and quickly expended fuels that

An entirely new form of energy transforms the old rocket-style spaceships into strange and alien shapes. This starship flies high above the gigantic Olympus Mons situated in the Amazonia Planitia region of Mars. The ancient volcano rises 15 miles above the surrounding plains and is the tallest mountain in the solar system.

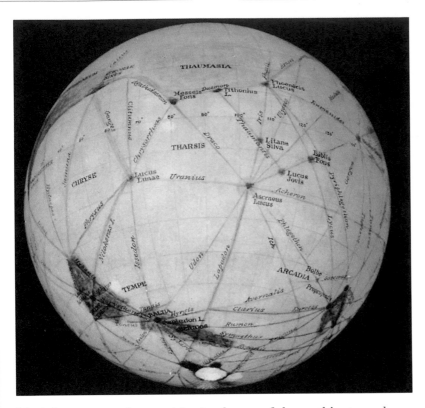

lifted the moon rockets so laboriously out of the earth's atmosphere. The new form of propulsion will create the possibility of much longer and more economical space travel. "Near to the great age a new power" may indicate that test runs will be undertaken before the trip to Mars, perhaps once again using our old friend the moon as the testing ground. The new power system will become increasingly successful between the period of 2nd August 1995 and 2nd May 1998. By 2000 the new technology will be extensively in use.

Research development begins on 3rd February 1992 and continues until 3rd February 1998 with ever increasing reward.

The dates 4th August to 4th September 2000 may designate the stay on Mars. Nostradamus indicates that the new process continues to use rockets but that the technology may require much smaller ones – the entire craft then being able to land on the planet. No claim is made for any one country – perhaps because it is a joint global operation.

At the beginning of the century the astronomer, Percival Lowell, produced detailed maps of Mars showing what he supposed to be a great artificial system of canals. These, of course, turned out to be a hopeful optical illusion but his idea of life on Mars could turn out to be less of a fantasy.

"Aliens Televized." — August 1998

Drawn from verse 1.42

    d   d   d   c

Personne télévise à chemin étrangers / intelligents du ciel du semblant

               h   d   d   l

cassé, boiteux. Les fera fuire. Rapatrie quoiqu'ils / remanient ca la croyance.

"On a road someone televizes intelligent aliens from the sky with a broken, limping appearance. He (or she) will put them to flight. He sends them home, although here they alter belief."

Time-Signal

d	d	d	c	h	d	d	l
r	n	n	e	r	r	r	y
4	4	4	3	8	4	4	11
17	13	13	5	17	17	17	23
4	4	4	3	8	4	4	2
8	4	4	5	8	8	8	5
	20		9	8	8		
						6	
	20	19	9	8	Aug	Aug	5

Many so called abductees agree the head of the alien shown above represents a recognizable portrait of space visitors who supposedly regularly visit earth. Many of those who claim to have seen such creatures often remember under hypnosis, experiments, abductions and meetings with these remarkable aliens. Will the TV image be anything like this reconstruction made under the direction of Whitley Strieber in his book Communion?

THIS UNIQUE AND PERHAPS TRAUMATIC EVENT seems to be reflected in the rather unusual time-signal chart. The date given for the encounter is August 1998 and the number "20" may refer to the number of aliens caught on film. There is some doubt about the day-date but this may be taken to be 5th August, while the first showing of the film is likely to be 6th August 1998.

Despite the fact that this sounds like something out of a science-fiction movie, the prediction follows all the rules we have established and can therefore be taken as seriously as any other prediction.

Someone, perhaps an amateur camera-person, happens across a group of creatures which evidently appear to be aliens "from the sky" while on a road on Earth. Nostradamus goes so far as to describe the beings as having a "broken, limping" movement which we may take either to be associated with alien biology or an injury. The aliens flee and return to their home world but the capturing of the images on film alters public opinion in regard to the existence of alien or extra-terrestrial life which has hitherto been a bone of considerable contention all over the world with many reports and conflicting information from sometimes very convincing sources.

Nostradamus gives us no information about the location of this encounter, except that it is on a road somewhere. The French word "casse" can also mean "cracked voice" so that we may also hear sounds of the aliens on the film.

Two images which evoke the popular idea of alien space craft. On the right artist Tim White perfectly captures the flying saucer myth. *Above:* A vast mothership hovers over Devil's Tower, Wyoming, in Spielberg's film, Close Encounters of the Third Kind.

RELIGION & MYSTICISM

"A New World Religion" – April 1993

Drawn from verse I.42

d   v

Le lendemain millième le Christianisme fait face à l'étrange doctrine /

  b   **b**   **t**   **o**   **a**

qu'encercle science et religion, deux hauts associés du Dieu / qui pat de

  l

sape.

"In the next millennium, Christianity faces a strange doctrine which encircles science and religion, two high associates of a God who suffers from undermining."

Time-Signal

d m	v i	b e	b c	t t	o o	a e	l e
4	21	2	2	19	14	1	11
12	1:9	5	3	1:9	1:9	5	5
4	3	2	2	19	5	1	2
3	19	5	3	19	19	5	5
4	193	2	Feb			1	Feb
Mar		May	3	2000	Aug		
						195	5

*Above:*Muslim girls praying in an Indonesian village. Islam is rapidly overtaking Christianity as the largest religious order in the world. But both remain "Religions of the Book", sharing with Judaism beliefs which were written as long as four millennia ago. They all rely on the sanctity of age as hallmarks of their authenticity. Any new religion will be one born in an age of information and science and is not likely to rely on the accuracy of scribes. *Far right:* A Voodoo priest of Haiti.

BEGINNING 4TH MARCH 1993, Nostradamus sees the rise of a new world religion to be at its peak during the coming millennium. The last major world religion to appear came 1,500 years ago – the beliefs of Islam. Because the dating mechanism in this volume only covers the years up to 2001, the period of the next millennium cannot be dated but described verbally only. (Nostradamus evidently divided his coding process according to centuries and millennia. For further details see last section)

The new religious doctrine will challenge Christianity by combining science and religion as part of one creed and from this meltdown

we can gather that the period between 2nd February and 3rd May 2000 is a significant time for the new growth of belief.

Christianity has been seriously undermined in the last centuries by the uneasy association of religion and a science which seems to reveal a mechanistic universe without a spiritual dimension. The presence in Christianity of a distant God has also brought dissatisfaction to a growing intelligence among the young and old alike who look for a more personal creed that brings God into the presence of humanity rather than one that punishes in life and promises only bliss after death.

In this respect Christianity will be seriously threatened as a religious and spiritual force between 1st February and 5th August 1995. Other predictions, such as the falling of the Christian Rome given earlier in this book, also add force to the predicted changes in religion.

"Osho Rajneesh." 1994 – 1995

Drawn from verse III.65

              r   **l**

Osho Rajneesh, un guru raréfie, empoisonné, rapproche deux pays. Peu à

        g   **r**   **d n**

peu, son mouvement luit / avec plus éclat en l'Inde et Amerique.

      r

Son sang sera dessus.

*"Osho Rajneesh, a thin, poisoned guru brings together two countries.
Little by little, his movement shines more brightly in India and America.
His blood will be upon it."*

Time-Signal

r h	l x	g m	r p	d t	n m	r e
17	11	7	17	4	13	17
8	? 22	12	15	19	12	5
8	2	7	8	4	4	8
8	4	3	6	19	3	5
98			8	194	Dec	
8	Apr		June		193	5
Aug	4	93				

OSHO RAJNEESH was the leader of a spiritual movement which created two experimental communities in Oregon, America, and Poona in India. His teachings against organized religion were regarded as highly controversial. Prior to his deportation in 1985, he was imprisoned and subsequently claimed that he had been poisoned by American government agents during this period.

"Thin" describes his emaciated appearance during his last years in India and Nostradamus appears to confirm he was indeed poisoned, although by what or whom is not clear.

During the period between 4th August 1993 and 8th April 1998 India and America are drawn closer together by the followers which he left, known as sannyasins. This period begins soon after the predicted earthquake in America and may herald a change of heart in the American authorities towards Eastern mystical teaching. America is destined to undergo great spiritual change during the next decade.

This revitalized relationship between the peoples of Osho and the American authorities will come about as a result of events during the period between 8th June 1993 and 5th December 1994. "His blood will be upon it" suggests that it is admitted that Rajneesh was deliberately given a slow-acting poison as a result of pressure on the authorities by the fundamentalist Christians who objected to his teachings.

Previous page: Osho Rajneesh helped by one of his disciples during a convalescence after his imprisonment in the U.S.A. *Above:* His body is carried to the funeral pyre in Poona, India, 1990. Substantial evidence has been gathered which shows he was poisoned with a slow acting radioactive substance while being held in custody in America.

"Women Priests in the Church of England."
1992-1998

Drawn from verse X.22

>   o   o   i
> *Archevêque de Canterbury consacre les femmes, prêtres. L'Eglise*
>   o   s   r   s   i   u   i   y
> *Anglicane / si auréolé. Voire, / quasi sourire poli du pape / donne signe*
>   r   a   i
> *du soin / que se nuit.*

"The Archbishop of Canterbury consecrates women priests. The Church of England greatly glorified. Indeed, a polite half-smile from the Pope shows a sign of concern that harms him."

Time-Signal

o / b	o / m	i / t	o / e	s / l	r / e	s / e	i / l	u / e	i / e	y / e	r / q	a / e	i / t
14	14	1:9	14	18	17	18	1:9	20	1:9	23	17	1	1:9
2	12	19	5	11	5	5	1	5	5	5	16	5	19
5	5	19	5	9	8	9	19	2	19	5	8	1	19
2	3	19	5	2	5	5	11	5	5	5	7	5	19
5 May			195		98	Sept		192		195	8 Jan*		
2 Mar			195	Feb	5	12			May	5	July	5	1991
				Aug									
				92	5								

* Here, 8th January most likely refers to 1992.

DECISION WILL SOON BE TAKEN within the Church of England establishment to admit women priests. The first two groups will be ordained by the Archbishop of Canterbury himself on 2nd March and 5th May 1995 to demonstrate the authority of the Church behind its decision.

Between 5th August 1992 and 5th February 1998 the Church of England is exalted by the prospect of this influx into the priesthood, possibly drawing larger congregations and numbers of women applicants for holy orders.

Between 12th September 1992 and 5th May 1995 the papacy becomes secretly alarmed, perhaps by the thought that women worshipers will be more drawn to a Church which has many women priests than to one which has none. It tries to disguise its apprehension with a polite, somewhat patronizing, attitude.

This policy is not successful, because Pope John Paul II has already made his position clear, perhaps with statements of opposition issued during the period 5th July 1991 and 8th January 1992.

Barbara Harris is consecrated in Boston as the first woman bishop in the United States. While such a progressive lead is given by America the clergy of the Church of England are known to be as conservative and reactionary as the Papacy. If this bastion of male supremacy falls to women then the Pope may well feel his own power slipping.

"AIDS in the Catholic Priesthood." 1992

Drawn from verse I,35

> **y**   **u**   **u**   **y**
> *La maladie AIDS en la prêtrise catholique. / Les homesexuels corromptent*
>   **y u**   **x u**
> *les juvéniles. / L'urne prétend que, vu leur vie à Croix, c'est mal.*
>   **i u**
> */ Le clergé ruiné, bagnard.*

"The disease AIDS in the Catholic priesthood. Homosexuals corrupt juveniles. The urn/ballot box asserts that, considering their life dedicated to the Cross, it is evil. The clergy destroyed, convict."

Time-Signal

y a	u t		u h	y t		y t	u q	u o	x t	u a		i e	u a
23	20		20	23		23	20	20	22	20		1:9	20
1	19		8	19		19	16	14	19	1		5	1
4	2		2	5		5	2	2	4	2		19	2
1	19		8	19		19	7	5	19	1		5	1
4	192		2	195		195		4	194	2			Feb
Jan			Aug				Dec			Jan		195	1
						Sept							
						197		5					

AFTER 4TH JANUARY 1992 the Roman Catholic Church will no longer be able to disguise the numbers of their priests who are both HIV positive and already developing the AIDS disease.

By 2nd August 1995 many juveniles (both male and female?) will have been sexually infected by a priesthood, one of whose primary vows is that of celibacy.

Because *l'urne* has two meanings, Nostradamus is possibly refer-ring to two social developments. Firstly, the deaths of many young

people will persuade society that their corruption by priests is not only immoral, but evil. Secondly, an electoral process will introduce legislation with severe penalties against knowingly infecting another person. Dates indicated are 2nd January 1994 and between 4th December 1995 and 5th September 1997.

As a result, from 1st February 1995 many priests are not only socially ruined, but imprisoned.

HEALTH, DISEASE AND SOCIETY

"Sound Waves Kill Cancer." – 1992 – 1998

Drawn from verse III.65

h   j   u

Après repartition donne la fréquence single pour agir sur malades, vagues de

u   u   a   y   h e u

son tuent/les cancers. Deviennent mous./ Leurs poisons partent / de corps.

"*After assessment gives the unique frequency to operate on the patients, waves of sound kill the cancers. They become lifeless. Their poisons leave the body.*"

Time-Signal

h t	j n	u n	u t	u s	a t	y i	h t	e d	u c
8	10	20	20	20	1	23	8	5	20
19	13	13	19	18	19	1:9	19	4	3
8	1	2	2	2	1	5	8	5	2
19	4	4	19	9	19	19	19	4	3
			(=10)						
									Feb
2 Jan 1992				92	191	195	198		93
4 Oct 1994									
1 Feb 1998									

THE CLINICAL RENDITION of this meltdown befits both the description of the medical treatment described and the profession of the prophet, who was himself a physician during his lifetime. New methods of cancer treatment will develop over the six years between 1992 – 1998. Important dates are 2nd January 1992, 4th October 1994 and 1st February 1998. First experiments indicate that sound waves leave cancer growths lifeless. These take place between 1991-2. The treatment becomes more and more successful during 1995-98, with the residues of cancer leaving patients completely cured. February 1993 may prove to be a turning point.

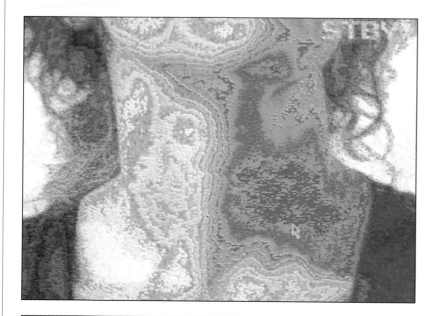

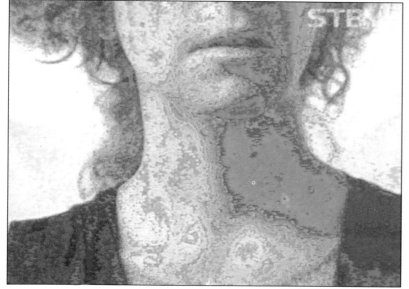

There are many hi-tech, alternative, diagnostic techniques available at present. The images here, for instance, show a patient before and after electro-crystal therapy, one of the many treatments which utilize color as a therapeutic tool. The top computer generated image shows the patient before treatment. According to the therapist the red "kundalini" energy is misplaced in the throat chakra. This can cause health problems. After color therapy the area around the throat is predominantly a blue and beneficial energy and correct for that region of the body. Similar treatment with sound could open up an entirely new therapy technique.

Medical experiments and diagnostic tests will fix the precise and unique sound frequency at which individual cancers may be killed. This may well include a kind of tissue typing, both of the cancer and the individual patient.

"Medicine Reverses the Ageing Process." – 1991-1998

Drawn from verse I.35

       c y

La médicine nouvelle traite la maladie d'âge; les vieux, jeunes crûs avec

r   y   l r   i   r u

peau lisse. Les séniles/perdent confusion./ Luxe robotique. Un/ rythme pur

  l   l

rue grumeaux.

"New medical treatments for the disease of ageing; the old, grown young with smooth skin. The senile lose their confusion. Robotic luxury. A pure rhythm kicks at lumps."

CHILDHOOD

Time-Signal

c e	y a	r a	y s	l t	r f	i t	r n	u t	l e	l e
3	23	17	23	11	17	1:9	17	20	11	11
5	1	1	18	19	6	1:9	13	19	5	5
3	5	8	5	2	8	19	8	2	2	2
5	1	1	9	19	6	19	4	19	5	5
Mar	13		95	Feb	8		198	195 9th Feb		
May	1		91		196		194	7th April,		
								5th June		
								or 195 + 5 = 2000		
								4th Feb		
								2nd April		

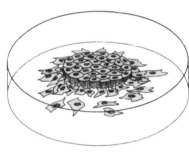

MATURITY

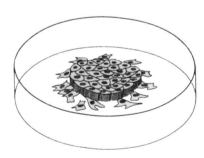

OLD AGE

ONE OF THE SOCIAL PROBLEMS of the nineties will be the older population of Western countries. Much emphasis will be placed on finding new treatments to reverse or halt the ageing process. According to Nostradamus, this research will prove successful. Successful tests allowing physical rejuvenation will come first between 1st May 1991 – 13th March 1995.

These fibroplasts, growing out of living tissue placed in a culture medium, demonstrate the diminishing ability of cells to replace and reproduce themselves with age.

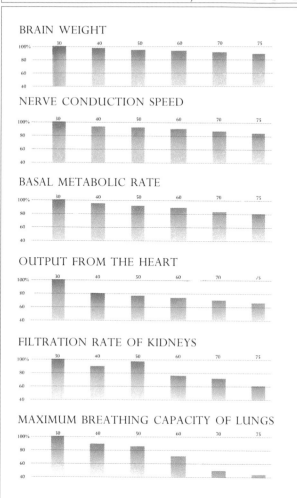

BRAIN WEIGHT

NERVE CONDUCTION SPEED

BASAL METABOLIC RATE

OUTPUT FROM THE HEART

FILTRATION RATE OF KIDNEYS

MAXIMUM BREATHING CAPACITY OF LUNGS

The six graphs show the decreasing efficiency of different organs in the human body as they age. These are plotted from 30 to 75 years of age and show a fall of range of between 9% for brainweight to 57% efficiency of the lungs.

This will be followed by treatment for senility which eliminates mental confusion with a medical advance on 8th February 1996. In general, many medical treatments at present carried out by doctors and nurses will be conducted by machines in luxurious surroundings (1994-8). The final statement is the most intriguing – possibly cancers will be disintegrated by a method of regular sound waves or vibrations (as described in the previous verse), individual patients being allocated their own "frequency" after assessment. We also see in the time-signal a succession of dates between 1995-2000, all of which may be significant in the development of the process (see previous prediction).

"The Power of Genetics." – 1995

Drawn from verse X.22

La génétique donne pouvoir sur le corps humain par dresser une carte. /

                    o

      i   **i**   **y**   **a**

Indique coeur d'une cellule. / Rase virus isolé. / A cas soi, signe soigné

    i

   par foyer sis.

"Genetics gives power over the human body by making a map. It indicates the heart of a cell. It destroys the isolated virus. On the case itself, the symptom treated through the located center of infection."

Time-Signal

o t	i e	i l	y e	a e	i e
14 19	1:9 5	1:9 2	23 5	1 5	1:9 5
5 19	19 5	19 2	5 5	1 5	19 5
195	195	192	May 5	Jan 5	195

THE HUGE TASK OF CHARTING a blueprint of the genetic structure of the human body has already begun. It has been estimated that it will take ten years, but Nostradamus states that this extra knowledge will help to heal many medical conditions by 1995. In that year the internal structure – "the heart" of each cell will be defined. From 5th May 1992 to January 1995 new treatments using genetic techniques will have begun to isolate and destroy viruses within the living cell. At present many medical conditions can only be treated by suppressing the symptoms with drugs. By 1995 the true cause of symptoms will be located and corrected within the genetic structure itself.

Diagram of the Human cell. At the center is the nucleus containing 23 pairs of chromosomes made up of thousands of genes, each coding an individual protein. The labyrinthine structure which surrounds it is a vital pathway for enzymes and hormones moving within the cell, while the small bean-like shapes are the mitochondria.

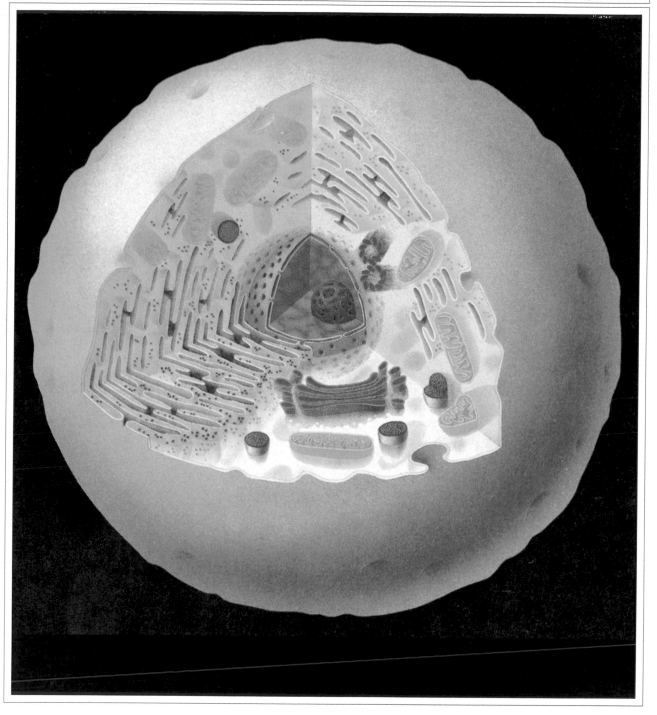

"Education." – 1994 – 1996

Drawn from verse I.42

>   **d**   **s**   **b**   **i**   **h**
> *Chaque enfant recoit l'education single. / Moniteurs ne gêner pas*
>   **a**   **s**   **dd**   **i**   **e**
> *cerveau. S'apprend loix / tellement beaucoup plus facilement / qu'il*
>   **i**   **i**
> *distance adultes.*

"Each child receives a unique education. The instructors will not constrict the brain. It teaches itself laws so much more easily that it outstrips adults."

Time-Signal

d	s	b	i	h	a	s	d	d	i	e	i
u	o	u	e	t	p	n	p	p	n	u	n
4	18	2	1:9	8	1	18	4	4	1:9	5	1:9
20	14	20	5	19	15	13	15	15	13	20	13
4	9	4	19	8	1	9	4	4	19	5	19
2	4	2	5	19	6	4	6	6	4	2	4
Apr		Apr		198	1					May	
2	94	2	195		June	94	1	1	194	2	194
				Aug 1					(95 twice)		
				196							

IN ALL THE SOCIAL CHANGES which Nostradamus describes and certainly with respect to education, the dates given, although significant in themselves, also mark a point when we will witness a new development and its continuing impact on society.

Children will receive individual attention in schools in such a way as to encourage a unique education, designed to draw out latent talents and creativity. Between 2nd April 1994 and 2nd April 1995 an educational pilot scheme may be introduced. Its results are then favorably assessed and the experiment becomes much more widespread between 1 August 1996 – 1 June 1998.

Back in the 1950's children had active and creative means of expression. Even poor children, as shown in the photograph, managed to devise complex games with only a piece of chalk. By the late 1970's and early 1980's over exposure to packaged concepts offered by television coupled with its almost hypnotic radiant light source has seriously impaired a whole generation's ability to construct abstract ideas. By the 1990's government authorities admit that the education system has all but collapsed and that 80% of children in the U.S. today are under- educated and unlikely to meet even the most modest requirements of industry.

The "instructors" in this scheme do not constrict the growing brain's learning abilities as may have been the case in previous educational systems. It is as though the chemical and electrical make-up of a child's brain receiving this new teaching is found to be physically different from that of a child receiving a conventional education. Nostradamus indicates that it learns "laws" rather than facts which it can then apply to a wide field of study.

As early as the initial scheme of 1994-5, it becomes clear that the new teaching methods enable children to learn at a rapid rate. On 2nd May 1994, only a month after the beginning of the scheme, children evidently compete with and even begin to outstrip adults.

It may be that the "instructors" are computers equipped with specially created learning programs based on individual assessments. Each child will have its own "school" entirely devoted to developing his or her abilities. New methods of fast learning now being pioneered in the States may also be involved.

THE FAR EAST

"Hong Kong and China" — 1995-6

Drawn from verse III.65

>   **n**   **d**
> *Aprés Russie se rend dur empire, en sequelles les Chinois se radoucent*
> **u**   **a**   **j**   **c**   **s**   **o**   **p**   **y**
> *gouverner sur leur/tenants. Hongkong/pourra fié. Pape aux Anglais./*
>   **e**
> *Hume va à foi.*

"After Russia gives up her harsh empire, in the aftermath the Chinese soften the government of their tenants. Hong Kong will be trusted. A pope among the English. Hume goes with faith to the foe."

Time-Signal

n r	d h	u g	a e	j s	c k	s f	o a	p x	y i	e i
13	4	20	1	10	3	8	14	15	23	5
17	8	7	5	18		6	1	22	1:9	1:9
4	4	2	1	1	3	9	5	6	5	5
8	8	7	5	9		6	1	4	19	19
Apr	4		6	91 Mar				6	195	195
8	Aug	9			193			Apr		
							May			
						96	1			

RUSSIA HAS GIVEN UP her "harsh empire". Possibly a loose confederation of new nation-states has been formed.

    Following the Russian example, China relaxes her hostility towards Hong Kong, which is free to continue as a capitalist economy. Dating indicates that China's government mellows considerably from its former orthodox communism between 4th April – 8th August 1995-6.

Previous page: Hong Kong in 1990
compared with the colony in 1967
(opposite) shows the massive
expansion area with the threat of the
Chinese takeover.

Hong Kong is "a tenant" – Nostradamus is aware that the official handover of the colony by Britain does not occur until 1997.
("K" is omitted because it is not an element of the numerical alphabet. "3" refers to the three countries of the United Kingdom which
form the British Crown governing Hong Kong prior to the handover to China).

Between March 1991 – 1993 Hong Kong will begin to be trusted by her future Chinese masters. Her economic future becomes
much more secure.

It becomes clear that before long a new pope will have come on
the scene. Possibly John Paul II is ailing at this time.

Britain's Cardinal Hume, Archbishop of Westminster, will
become the next pope in 1995. (See Religion predictions). The
period here is 6th April 1995 to 1st May 1996, although other predictions suggest January or October 1995. The numbers 6 and 4 in
the set above add up to 10 or 1, possibly also referring to either
October or January. Therefore October is more likely because it
falls within this period.

"Hume goes with faith to the foe" ("a" in French means both
"with" and "to") may describe a peace mission undertaken by the
new pope to southern Europe in 1995 (see EUROPE predictions).
If 195 also refers to October this means he would depart on or by
the 5th of the month (19 = 1:9 = 10 = October 5 = 5th).

"China Survives Alone." – 1991 – 1995

Drawn from verse III.65

   u   q   y   r

La Chine dure seule, ourlée a démocraties. / On ménage rapports.

   s   u   u   f

Juin/ Pont cassé nuire à son voisin le Japon. Le pire/ des vagues

   d   r   h

énormes fera tuer nageurs.

"China survives alone, hemmed in by democracies. Relationships are handled with care.

   June – the `broken bridge' will harm her neighbor Japan. The worst of huge waves will kill swimmers."

Time-Signal

| u | q | y | r | s | u | u | f | d | r | r | h |
a	e	i	s	j	o	e	i	m	f	t	r
20	16	23	17	18	20	20	6	4	17	17	8
1	5	1:9	18	10	14	5	1:9	12	6	19	17
2	7	5	8	9	2	2	6	4	8	8	8
1	5	19	9	1	5	5	19	3	6	19	8
9		195	98		Feb 2		196	12		198	8
1	May			91	5	May			Sept		
											Aug

ETWEEN MAY 1991 AND 1995 China sees her former communist allies becoming democracies in the new world order. She survives for the time being as the last communist state, but handles these new relationships with sensitivity between 1991 and 1998, indicating a significant event at the beginning of this period.

Student flags in Peking, China. This demonstration in 1990 was put down by the authorities as ruthlessly as ever, with many of the leaders being given harsh sentences, apparently to dissuade others who might revolt.

The China Wall. Many commentators wonder how long China can resist the ideological and economic pressures of the democracies which surround her borders. As the last great outpost of communist power how long can China maintain her sense of splendid isolation?

Between 5th February and 5th May 1996 China's neighbor Japan bears an increasingly heavy burden. From other predictions we know that this arises from huge investment in an America which becomes economically unstable in the first half of the decade.

An earthquake in California is predicted elsewhere, as we have seen, for 8th May 1993. The reference to "the broken bridge" is the San Francisco bridge which will be destroyed. Hollywood will be devastated. The Japanese have recently begun buying up leading Hollywood film companies.

This could be regarded as a localized disaster, if it were not for the fact that in the years following the earthquake the base of American power, her agriculture, is ruined by climatic change. Between 8th August and 12th September 1998 Japan's economy becomes fragile and many suffer as a result.

This seems to be an economic warning rather than a literal one, because of the precise information given in the next prediction, "Japan's Economy Hurt". But it is possible that, following the earthquake, the "Ring of Fire" – volcanoes and earthquake regions surrounding the Pacific Ocean – will be highly disturbed, sending out huge tsunami or giant waves over a vast region in which Japan is included.

"Japan's Economy Hurts." – 1993 - 1996

Drawn from verse III.65

    o   **d**   **s**   **o**   **s**

L'économie du Japon sera mal affecté / par le séisme grand / en

    u   **n**   **o**   **v**   **p**   **o**

l'Amerique. / Le pire su n'est passé. / Agriculture – vue en ruine. / Yen

  h   **u**   **p** **h**

fragile dure sac. Nus se noyer.

"Japan's economy will be badly affected by the great earthquake in America. This is not the worst knowledge. Agriculture (America's) – a ruined sight. The fragile yen endures pillage. Those unprotected will drown themselves."

Time-Signal

o	d	s	o	s	u	n	o	v	p	o	h	u	p	h
i	f	l	m	e	m	e	a	l	e	i	f	c	e	y
14	4	18	14	18	20	13	14	21	15	14	8	20	15	8
1:9	6	11	12	5	12	5	1	11	5	1:9	6	3	5	23
5	4	9	5	9	2	4	5	3	6	5	5	2	6	8
19	6	2	3	5	3	5	1	2	5	1:9	1:9	3	5	5
May	4													
	196													
195	4		95		92			Mar	6	195	195		8	Aug
	June	Feb	3	May	3	95	Jan	2	May			193	5	May
		May		Feb										
		92	3	95	3									

THIS PROPHECY READS like an economic report – about the future. America's current deficit in the early nineties is massive. Uncontrollable circumstances add to this burden until America's economy is broken. From the California earthquake, due on 8th May 1993, Japan can no longer play "angel", because the demands on her economy become such that even this technological giant of the post-war world cannot sustain the demands – 4th June 1995 - 4th May 1996. The economic damage sustained by the earthquake takes place earlier, between 3rd February 1992 and February

1995. These dates are repeated twice in the chart indicating that they affect America and Japan equally. Note that the damage begins to occur a year *before* the predicted earthquake, probably as investors "play safe" and begin to switch their holdings elsewhere.

Worse is to come after January 1995. Nostradamus predicts that America's agriculture is visibly ruined between 6th March and 2nd May 1995. The yen will be most vulnerable to financial attack between 5th May 1993 - 8th August 1995.

Tokyo Stock Exchange. The Japanese Yen remains the most stable and sought after currency even into the 1990's. But, linked as it is with the economy of the United States, this could become vulnerable if anything happened to its major market outlet.

AFRICA

"AIDS from Africa." – 1993

Drawn from verse III.65

                      n

AIDS pullule en Mediterranee d'Afrique. Sang sera navigué, volé. La peste

       n   **u**   **s**   **n**   **g**

rase Roma. Pontife/prie. Scythe rouvre Europe au sud – / pan. Nord;

j   **h**

soucis sur océan.

"AIDS swarms in the Mediterranean from Africa; blood will be navigated and flown. The plague brings down Rome. The Pope prays. A scythe reopens a section in the south of Europe. In the north, concerns over the ocean."

Time-Signal

n	n	u	s	n	g	j	h
v	i	t	r	a	d	i	a
13	13	20	18	13	7	10	8
21	1:9	21	17	1	4	1:9	1
4	3	2	9	4	7	1	8
3	19	3	8	1	4	19	1
4	193	Feb	98	Apr	7	191 + 9 = 2000
Mar		3		1	Apr	

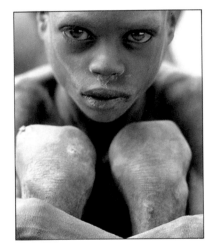

LITTLE PUBLICITY HAS BEEN GIVEN in the West to the devastating effects of AIDS in Africa which resembles a plague in the Middle Ages. By 4th March 1993, AIDS will be "swarming" in the Mediterranean. Nostradamus compares it with the gathering of millions of locusts to convey the magnitude of the problem. He knows the virus is carried in blood and other bodily fluids. Europe is unable to repel a disease silently arriving on every ship and aircraft. Rome is racked by this epidemic. So what is left? Only prayer. But the Pope, too, is destroyed.

Throughout these predictions Nostradamus makes constant references to war in southern Europe and the Middle East. (See EUROPE and MIDDLE EAST predictions). The scythe, a death symbol, points to Europe being attacked (3rd February 1998). Pan also identifies the oldest Greek god; Greece becomes vulnerable to an attack from a "scythe", possibly a disguised reference to Turkey.

| **n** | | | 13 |
| pan / section / Greece? | | | 1 |

This is a map reference. Reverse 13 to 31 and extend 1 to 10, add these together, we achieve the number 41.

41 degrees latitude crosses the map very near Istanbul, the capital of Turkey, traversing the Aegean Sea into northern Greece. This may mean that the attack comes from Turkey (1st – 7th April 1991).

Deep concerns arise over a section of a northern ocean – the Arctic – which may show higher levels of pollution, or rising sea-levels

Prostitutes in Bangui laughingly show an 'AIDS Monster" poster. But the problem in Africa is anything but a joke and governments who simply cannot afford the costs of routine HIV tests are tardy in educating the population. Although condoms help prevent the spread of the syndrome many are Catholic communities and the Pope has banned their use. Caught between poverty and dogma the people of Africa will suffer terribly in the last decade of this millennium.

as the ice melts under the greenhouse effect, even a new hole in the ozone layer. One exists already over Antarctica.

g
Nord   13   14   17   4

With geographical directions, all numbers should be included.

$$
\begin{array}{llll}
 & & & 7 \\
13 & 14 & 17 & 4 \\
 & 27 & 44 & \\
71 & & & \\
71 & + & 74 & = 145 \\
\end{array}
$$

145 degrees longtitude by 71-74 degrees latitude fixes the location of the rising concern as the Arctic ocean.

Deep concern remains until the year 2000.

"Refugee Millions Die in Sudan." — 1998

Drawn from verse X.22

>   **c**   **n**   **r**   **r** **i**
> *Afrique — millions des gens refugiés voraces voyagent / au Soudan. Puis*
>   **i**   **s**   **i**   **i**   **d**   **r**
> */ mises au / lieux où meurent, / corps à soir, sinon ceux-là qu' /*
>   **o**   **i**   **r**
> *échappent rôder à / l' / Egypte.*

*"Africa — millions of voracious refugees travel to the Sudan. Then they
are put in places where they die, corpses by the evening, except those who
escape to wander about Egypt."*

Time-Signal

c e	n g	r f	r t	i a	s m	i x	i m	i p	d x	r u	o t	i l	r t
3	13	17	17	1:9	1:9	18	1:9	1:9	4	17	14	1:9	17
5	7	6	19	1	12	22	12	15	22	20	19	11	19
3	4	8	8	19	19	9	19	19	4	8	5	19	8
5	7	6	19	1	3	4	3	6	4	2	19	2	19
Mar 12				191	193	94	193	194		8	195		
12 June 198								196	4 Feb			192198	

T HE DATING SYSTEM in this prediction alters the whole sense
of the message. Between 12th March and 12th June 1998 in
Africa, millions of starving refugees are on the move. The
build-up to this situation begins in 1991 in Sudan where attempts
will be made to marshal the refugees and place them in camps
(1993-4). From 8th February 1994 to 4th February 1996 a huge
number die in less than a day (which suggests, among other causes, an uncontrollable epidemic). A number escape over the border
with Egypt in 1995. Between 1992-8 Egypt is severely affected by
the refugee problem in Sudan on her southern frontier.

Already in 1990 this situation began to build up. Millions face
death from famine in Sudan and Ethiopia because the rains have
failed in the Horn of Africa.

Refugees in Ethiopia 1990. Few
Western nations have any concept
of the sheer numbers involved in
the African tragedy. It is not a
matter of thousands dying of
hunger, disease and AIDS but of
tens of thousands. By the end of
this decade Nostradamus predicts
that these numbers will
dramatically rise to hundreds of
thousands and even millions.

A U S T R A L A S I A

"A Fight for Rights." – 2000

Drawn from verse III.65

> p   c   r   r   s   o
> *L'Australie / sent durer ouragans, du furieux peuple / aborigéne,*
> s   h   s   s   s   c
> *pendant / qu'en Nouvelle-Zélande / le / gouvernement / pose honneurs*
> y   j
> *aux Maoris pacifiques.*

"Australia will experience lasting political storms from a furious aboriginal people, while in New Zealand the government treats the pacific Maoris honorably."

Time-Signal

p l	c i	r u	r x	s u	o b	s e	h q	s z	s l	s t	c n	y x	j s
15	3	17	17	18	14	18	8	18	18	18	3	23	10
11	1:9	20	22	20	2	5	16	24	11	19	13	22	18
6	3	8	8	9	5	9	8	9	9	9	3	5	1
2	19	2	4	2	2	5	7	6	2	19	4	4	9
6	193	8	Aug	92	May		Aug		92	199	Mar	5	9:1 = 10
Feb			Feb	4	2	95	7	96			4	Apr	

* The combination 9:1 = 10 refers to the year 2000 (90 + 10 = 100), rather than 1991, although time may prove differently. This conclusion is reinforced by the appearance of 1999 just before this section.

Map Reference:

> y   j
> *aux Maoris pacifiques*
> 23   10 = 1
> 22   18

Previous page: Demonstration for Aboriginal rights in Sydney, Australia. *Right:* Maori women singing during the Royal Jubilee Tour at Gisbourne, New Zealand.

With the treaty possibly taking effect in the year 2000, the final thought is that these numbers could also be map references.

$$23 + 22 = 45 \qquad 18 - 1 = 17 = 170$$

45 degrees latitude cuts across the southern end of New Zealand's South Island, while 170 degrees longitude divides the island roughly in two.

COULD NOSTRADAMUS BE ATTEMPTING to offer a location for newly acquired territorial lands for the Maori nation under a treaty with the New Zealand government?

The problems could be about land rights of indigenous peoples, the aborigines in Australia and the Maoris in New Zealand.

The Australian government (6th February 1993, possibly the date of a general election) is "harsh" towards its aborigines' claims for which they are campaigning. This refusal to deal unleashes political storms, perhaps even violent resistance from 4th February to 8th August 1992. This comes to a head on 2nd May 1995.

In New Zealand the government treats the Maoris honorably – perhaps offering a treaty which recognizes the Maoris as a sovereign nation with territorial rights – 7th August 1996. This was the solution adopted by the American government to end the Indian wars of the last century. Possibly land approximating to 45 degrees latitude, 170 degrees longitude will be ceded in perpetuity to the Maoris. The process of recognizing the sovereignty of the Maori nation continues from 1992-9, with the process being completed during the year 2000 between 5th March and 4th April.

Nostradamus describes the Maoris as *pacifiques* – members of the great sweep of Polynesian peoples which migrated through the Pacific ocean and settled on its numerous islands. But *pacifiques* also means "calm" – Maori leaders do not adopt the violent tactics of the aborigines, whose history is one of suffering and decimation at the hands of white settlers.

SCIENCE & ECOLOGY

"A Poisoned Earth." – 1995

Drawn from verse III.65

>   **n**   **p**
> *Roi Charles, l'homme fié éprouvé de grand travail / sentinelle*
>   **n**   **y**   **o j**   **p**
> *pour terre empoisonnée au scie, quand USA casse, fuse. Guerres –*
>   **au**
> *danger en Europe, sud en sus.*

"King Charles, the steadfast man tested by a great task – sentinel for an earth poisoned by the saw – when the USA cracks and crackles. War – danger in Europe, as well as to the south."

Time-Signal

n	p	n	y	o	j	p	a	u
m	e	e	i	e	f	r	d	e
13	15	13	23	14	10	15	1	20
12	5	5	1:9	5	6	17	4	5
4	6	4	5	5	1	6	1	2
3	5	5	19	5	6	8	4	5
Dec	4	195		5	Jan		9	
3	Oct			Nov	12		5	

Charles, the present Prince of Wales and heir to the British throne, is an ardent campaigner on behalf of the environment. He is unique amongst recent royalty in that he has both strong views on the ecology of the planet and the courage to voice them in public.

C HARLES III WILL RULE BRITAIN in this decade, but there is an even greater destiny unfolding for him - leader of the battle to save an earth "poisoned by the saw".

In this one phrase Nostradamus encapsulates all that is wrong with our planet. We have sawn down the trees, the lungs of the earth, which could have absorbed much of the pollution we have been putting out for decades.

The device *n/m* which appears in *l'homme fie* proves the lineage and therefore the identity of "King Charles".

3 = 2 = 5
1 = 1 = 2

In 1952, Queen Elizabeth II inherited the monarchy after the death of her father George VI. "2" in the device refers to Queen

Elizabeth the Second (II) and "3" to her eldest son, who will be Charles III. The device appears in the time-signal above.

Between 3rd October and 4th December 1995 Charles III takes on a leading role in the worldwide campaign to save the environment.

"When the USA cracks and crackles ... " *Casse* means "to crack like a nut" and must describe initially the great earthquake in 1993 (see AMERICA). One of the "cracks" may be the San Andreas fault, but California is criss-crossed with a multitude of such lines. "Cracking" may also refer to the fragmentation of American society under increased stress.

The center of conflict also refers to Europe as she finds herself threatened from within, as well as from the south.

Part of the danger may come from Sudan, according to certain letters in the phrases:

a u

sud, en sus _can be linked to the name "Sudan". (see Africa).

America is burning. Europe faces conflict. The crisis period is 5th January – 12th November 1995.

"A New Hole in the Ozone Layer." – 1993-1997

Drawn from verse III.65

s   g   s   p
Le grand Trou dure en niveau d'ozone sur l'Antarctique. / Ocean
s   s   p   l   a   p   p s
d'Arctique – encore un ouvre. / Il ménace à ruiner le monde / que ne
g   h   j
pare pas scythe, fosses fusés.

"*The Great Hole continues in the ozone layer over Antarctica. The Arctic ocean – another one opens up. It threatens to ruin the world, which cannot by itself avoid the crackling scythe, the crackling pits.*"

Time-Signal

s	g	s	p	s	s	p	l	a	p	p	s	g	h	j
z	s	t	c	q	c	e	c	e	d	q	n	a	t	f
18	7	18	15	18	18	15	11	1	15	15	18	7	8	10
24	18	19	3	16	3	5	3	5	4	16	13	1	19	6
9	7	9	6	9	9	6	2	1	6	6	9	7	8	10 or 1
6	9	19	3	7	3	5	3	5	4	7	4	1	19	6
			June		June		2	July		June		7	198	10 or 1
96	97	199	3	97	93	5	3	9		7	94		Jan	June

THIS PREDICTION warns that the entire world will be touched by the problems of the ozone hole in the atmosphere over Antarctica which will continue to cause concern from 1996 to 1999. But then we will see a new hole over the Arctic Ocean emerging and developing between 5th June 1993 and 3rd June 1997. This second hole will confirm to the world's scientists and ecologists just what is happening.

The reference to a "scythe" is an indication of the "cutting" power of heat over crops when the sun shines through a broken atmosphere.

The world cannot "by itself" avoid the consequences (from "ne" including "s", making the verb reflexive as well as negative). Perhaps Nostradamus offers us his help by predicting the new hole, giving humanity a chance to prepare. The problem begins on 7th June 1994 and continues to between 7th January and 10th June 1998. The device "J10" at the end of the time chart may indicate that the problem will continue for 10 years further into the year 2008.

The use of the word "fosses" may refer to the pits that are used to bury farm animals, thus pointing to large-scale slaughter or natural death of animals such as cattle, sheep and pigs who expire from heat and exhaustion or thirst and starvation or disease.

The use of the word "crackling" is likely to refer to widespread drought or global warming or perhaps even land-fires brought about by the excessive heat.

The overall message is that there is to be a greater threat to mankind from his own gradual corruption of the environment than from any potential war between nations. Ultimately, the predicted disasters could bring mankind together enough to make him forget his perpetual differences!

The greatest message that has come back from all the space missions is that the planet is an undivided whole. Whatever happens on one side of the globe can have far reaching consequences for the rest.

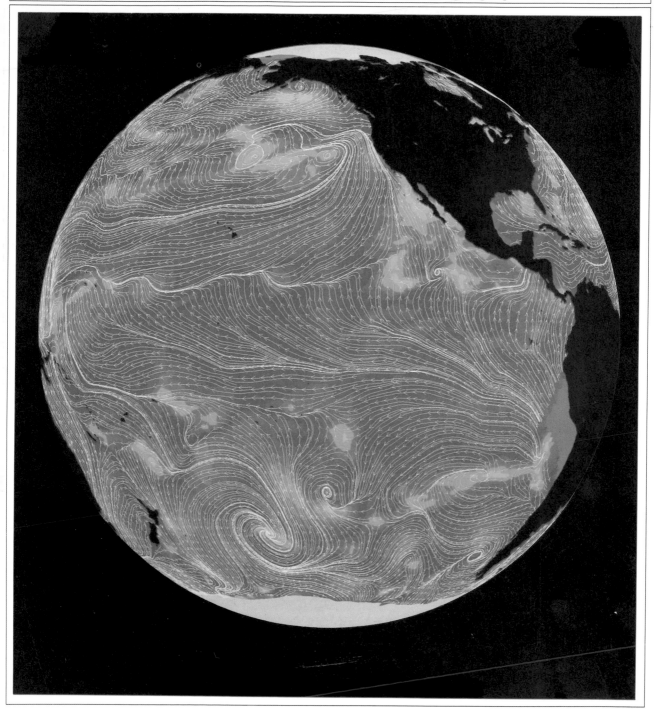

"The Black Hole Explained." – June 1995

Drawn from verse III.65

e

La physique nouvelle décrire trou noir. Après Juin, ère autre commence.

e

Elle a / porte./

e   p   s   h

Soudan, sas d'Afrique, va. En Nations-Unis peur des / groupes sanguins.

"The new physics will describe a black hole. After June, another era begins. It has a gateway.
    Sudan, the sieve of Africa, goes. Among the United Nations there is fear of blood groups."

Time-Signal

e i	g t	e q	p i	s e	h i
5	7	5	15	18	8
1:9	19	16	1:9	5	1:9
5	7	5	6	9	8
19	19	7	19	5	19
		5	196		198
195	197		July	95	

Right: Our present understanding of a black hole suggests that a star which collapses upon itself reaches a critical density which is greater than can be sustained in our universe. It then drops out altogether, leaving an empty black hole in space. Some scientists believe that these mysterious holes might be used as short cuts through space. Perhaps a practical method is devised to do this within the next few years.

I N THE 1990s PHYSICS WILL TAKE A GIANT LEAP forward with the emergence of a mathematical explanation of how a black hole functions. When a giant star dies, it collapses, its mass crushed by its own weight until it reaches the state of a "black hole" which has no mass, but enormous gravitational pull on its surroundings. Nothing, not even light, escapes this pull and there has been some speculation that anything entering the hole may somehow lead into another universe.

An astronaut falls into a black hole. The gravity at his feet would be millions of times greater than at his head. On entering the event horizon he would become an extended thin thread hundreds of kilometers in length.

A spacecraft approaches a black hole. Around the perimeter of the hole light from stars has been trapped into temporary orbit which makes it appear that there are millions of stars around the event horizon.

Nostradamus indicates that the explanation will be based on new theories of physics proposed after June 1995. These theories may involve a total explanation of how the universe functions – a fundamental advance in the understanding of the nature of matter initiating the Aquarian Age. There may in fact be some more esoteric result from the realization of the functions of the black holes – perhaps not only beginning a new scientific era but opening up mankind's own understanding of the psyche. The phrase "after June" might apply to the year 1997, in which case the number 197 can be interpreted to mean 19th July.

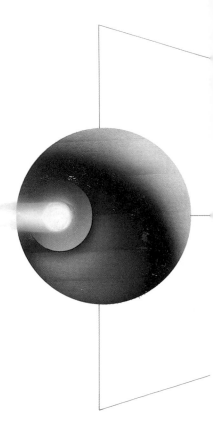

It is fascinating to note the way in which Nostradamus often divides his predictions into two parts – in this case concerned with black holes on one side and Sudan in Africa on the other – but uses similar imagery in both sections. The word "porte" can, if the "t" is taken out, be used instead to indicate the French word "Pore" which means "porous" or full of holes. An interesting theory might be that the universe is full of black holes in the same way as Nostradamus indicates that Sudan is the "sieve of Africa", and somehow these holes work in the same way as the pores in the human body. It has already been established that the planet Earth operates in this way.

From Sudan we can expect to see mass migration from 5th July 1996, as everything passes through the country – the sieve of Africa. In the same year the United Nations becomes concerned with "blood groups" or perhaps groups of blood, in any case certainly a connection with AIDS. The problem to be solved continues as a matter of debate between 1995 and 1998.

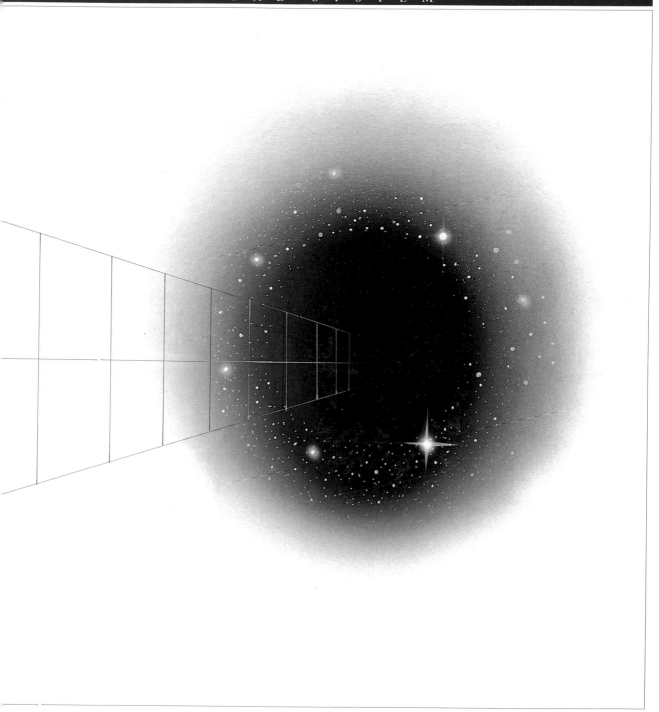

SECTION FIVE

THE SYSTEM REVEALED IN FULL

THE MURDER OF HENRY II OF FRANCE

IN ORDER TO GIVE THE READER a detailed explanation of the decoding system, we must turn to the past – to one of the most famous predictions that Nostradamus ever made – a prophecy made concerning an event that was to take place during his own life – one that came true while he lived, and linked him forever with the fortunes of the royal families of France. This event influences even our world today. First the story surrounding the event predicted.

In the year 1556, Catherine de Medici, wife of the French king Henry II, became deeply troubled by a prediction issued by an Italian astrologer she had known in her youth.

The prediction told of danger, blindness and possibly even death for Henry from any form of single combat during his forty-first year.

Catherine, like many of her contemporaries, was steeped in astrological culture and knew that such a warning could not be ignored. Nevertheless, she needed confirmation from an independent and, if possible, French source – particularly if the King had to be told of the prediction.

Catherine's mind worked in typically methodical fashion.

What could be a better solution than to summon to the capital the new prophet from the French Mediterranean south – one who had no connection with the French Court and – even more importantly – with Catherine herself?

This prophet had only the year before published a book of his own predictions, one of which had been specific about an accident

befalling a royal "lion" in a duel. The prediction had already caused disturbed whisperings in Paris.

So it was that a retired doctor living in Provence, who made his living by writing almanacs, received a royal summons he had long foreseen, a command to attend the Queen.

This month-long journey and its resultant meeting would forever link him with the event which caused the downfall of the Valois royal house and the immense historical changes which issued from it.

The text of the quatrain describing the circumstances of Henry II's death is unusually precise, because Nostradamus already knew when he wrote it that it contained the first prophecy to be fulfilled in *Siecles*, his book of predictions. *The Siecles*, or *Centuries*, were not published in full until after Nostradamus' death, but the quatrain describing Henry II's death in 1559 had been published in 1555.

In its original form, prophecy I.35 is still cited as one of his most extraordinary successes. It has continued to fire the reader's imagination over the centuries, as it was intended to do by the author himself. Compared with many other predictions that he made concerning more distant future events, the Henry II verse is very clear. It is as though he knew when he wrote it that it contained the first of his major prophecies which would come true during his life and that it should be understandable to all who read it.

The event it describes would come about during his own lifetime three years from the time of his journey to Paris. His prediction of it would place him in some danger and ensure that he did not again leave his native Provence.

But all that, as with so much in his life and work, was still in the future.

> *Le lyon ieune le vieux furmontera,*
> *En champ bellique par fingulier duelle,*
> *Dans cage d'or les yeux luy crevera,*
> *Deux claffes vne puis mourir mort cruelle.*
>
> I.35

This is the original form of the prophecy, with the archaic "f", instead of the letter "s" which we use today.

Some of the spelling is different, too. For example, *ieune/young* is spelled nowadays as *jeune*. *Luy/him* is now lui.

In addition, of course, the text is in old French, or Provence. The first task then, is to unlock the coded texts by modernizing the text without losing the essential elements which make up the verse as you see it now.

We change the medieval "f" to "s" and we correct some of the more outlandish spellings by putting the familiar letters in.

What we don't do is lose sight of the old letters. They go over the top of the new ones so that we are still aware of their presence. This is very important as these "left-over" letters are going to show us how to date the prophecy.

Let us work through the verse line by line with the literal English meaning of the line directly underneath.

>   **y i**
> *Le lion jeune le vieux surmontera*
> *The lion young the old will overcome*

> *En champ bellique par singulier duelle*
> *In field warlike by a remarkable duel*

>   **y u**
> *Dans cage d'or les yeux lui crevera,*
> *In cage of gold the eyes him will blind*

>   **v**
> *Deux classes une puis mourir mort cruelle.*
> *Two classes one then to die death cruel*
>
> I.35

Originally Nostradamus predicted two lines of fate for Henry II and the Royal House of Valois. He said that Henry could become the finest king since Charlemagne, healing the wounds between the warring religious factions of Catholic and Huguenot. He prophesied, however, that there was an alternative and tragic path of destiny on which Henry could die from a jousting "accident" which would bring the whole House of Valois to extinction within one generation.

It should be remembered that we are not here trying to translate the verse itself because it was never intended to be translated as such, but decoded. It was designed to remain as a verse simply as a device to divert the attention. All 942 the verses of *Siecles* were written for this reason in this form.

Nostradamus actually told us this himself in his Preface to *Siecles*, stating plainly that he had provided distorted versions of his original prophecies because society in the coming centuries was going to alter so much that the authorities of his time – Church, monarchy and nobility – would not find it possible to believe what he was telling them if the prophecies were too clearly uttered.

Remember, this is still the same verse, even though it now looks much more modern.

The text still appears confused, because the French is confused.

A normal French word like "duel" ends in this verse with an extra "le". This is not a mistake, but deliberately inserted. We will see the exciting use to which they can be put.

The young lion the old will overcome
In a warlike field by a remarkable duel,
In a cage of gold the eyes he will blind him,
Two classes one then to die cruel death.

Just why did this verse arouse so much controversy both at the time it was made and three years later when Henry II died (the verse is a prediction of his death, for those who are not familiar with Nostradamus' works)?

Although the verse remains confused, its descriptive imagery is striking. What concentrated interest on the prediction most was the reference to "a lion", for this was an occasional emblem of Henry II.

The prediction of Gauric, Catherine de Medici's childhood astrologer, was that Henry should beware of a single combat during his forty-first year which might bring about blindness and possibly death.

Gauric's prediction is very specific while Nostradamus' seems to skate around the subject. It describes an old and a young lion engaged in a duel in which one will overcome the other in a field of war. There are obscure references to a "cage of gold", blinded eyes, two "classes", then one will die a "cruel death". But there is nothing definite there; no factual statement, no real conclusions,

Catherine de 'Medici, 1519–1589 Catherine held power as Regent throughout the reigns of her sons, Francis II and Charles IX, only relenquishing that power during the reign of her third son, Henry III.

and, above all, no reference to age or indeed any date at all! Concentrating on this text is like trying to hold water in your hands, you can only do it for a few seconds, after which it runs away.

Nostradamus' verse contains dramatic images in abundance – that is his trademark – but not a single detail which could convince the reader that he was prophesying this event at all. And this has often been the failing of the prophet in the eyes of the modern reader. So many interpretations have been made of his work and many of them have simply turned out to be wrong because the literal verse has been taken as the basis for the interpretation. To the cynic therefore, there is nothing reliable upon which he can base his belief. But the real problem is not that we invariably seem to fail in our attempts to gather precise information from the Prophet's verses, but that we have not asked the right questions of his works – or indeed enough questions.

When Nostradamus arrived in Paris, he had a long audience with Queen Catherine, who remained impressed to the end of her life with his prophetic powers, and a briefer conversation with Henry, to whom, it is said, he explained the meaning of the prophecy above.

As will become clear, he could not have explained the *true and secret meaning*, otherwise the King might well have acted differently, history would have been irrevocably changed and none of Nostradamus' other predictions would have come true. Perhaps this needs a little deeper explanation.

Nostradamus' understanding of the future was that it was irrevocable – there were no "shoulds" or "coulds", nothing conditional – life either happened as it was destined or it did not happen at all. His vision of the future was literally split into two parts; one that was unchangeable, the events and people unaware of what was going to happen, and one that could be appreciated and acted upon. The first period was that time which would elapse from his own life until today, and the second period was from today onwards. Only once a deciphering code was learned would it be possible for mankind to appreciate his own future. Henry II could not, therefore, be allowed to know the true and secret meaning of the verses, for if he did, he might have altered all time to come. Nostradamus believed that only in the late 20th century would mankind possess sufficient intelligence to be able to handle his own future, and that the discovery of the correct code would come at precisely the right time. It is the contention of the authors that this time has now come.

After a stay of some weeks in the capital, during which he had the further delicate task of drawing up horoscopes for Catherine's several children (the ruling house of Valois would not survive beyond her four sons and the last daughter, wife of the Bourbon Henry IV, would die childless), Nostradamus was warned that the magistrates in Paris were making inquiries about his possible use of magical practices. Astrology was permitted, but magic was

not – a distinction which seems strange to us, but astrology was then regarded as a science.

He immediately left Paris and returned home.

Three years later, on 28 June 1559, a three-day tournament began in Paris to celebrate the double marriage of the King's daughters to Philip II of Spain and the Duke of Savoy.

Henry himself took part, delighting everyone with his skill.

On the afternoon of the third day he jousted with Count Montgomery, Captain of his Scottish Guard. They rode against each other twice, with no decisive result.

In their third encounter, the point of Montgomery's lance passed through the visor of the King's helm, piercing his eye, and Henry fell from his horse.

He lingered on in agony, his doctors powerless, until his death on July 10th.

The French Court and people were stunned. Henry was a vigorous, athletic man who had been expected to live for many more years. His eldest son, Francis, was only fifteen.

This tragic event took on a more disturbing aspect when it was realized that Nostradamus had prophesied the circumstances of Henry's death, word for word, in the edition of *Siecles* published four years before and one year before he had met the King in Paris.

Armed with this knowledge, we, as receivers of the prophecy, can now adjust the wording of the quatrain in line with the historical event.

We left the prophecy in this form:

> **y   i**
> *Le lion jeune le vieux surmontera*
> "The lion young the old will overcome"
> *En champ bellique par singulier duelle*
> "In field warlike by a remarkable duel"
> **y   u**
> *Dans cage d'or les yeux lui crevera,*
> "In cage of gold the eyes him will blind"
> **v**
> *Deux classes une puis mourir mort cruelle.*
> "Two classes one then to die death cruel"
> I.35

Above: Seventeen years after Montgomery's lance had pierced the eye of the king he returned to France as leader of a Huguenot uprising. He was captured and Catherine, now an older woman as in the painting, had him executed.

Previous page: The tournament in which Henry II received the fatal wound as Montgomery's lance pierced the golden visor of the king's helm. This tragic event marked the beginning of a series of diabolic intrigues, religious persecutions and assassinations which had far reaching effects across the whole of Europe.

In the light of our knowledge of the events we can adjust the text to look like this:

>   **i**   **y**
> *Le jeune surmontera le vieux lion. En champ bellique par singulier*
>   **y** **u**
> *duelle, lui crevera — "Les yeux dans cage d'or", deux classes, puis une*
>
> *mourir mort cruelle.*

In English then:
"The young man will overcome the old lion. In a warlike field by a remarkable duel, he will blind him — 'the eyes in a Golden Cage'; two training runs, then one will die a cruel death."

In a sense, we are cheating here because we know what happened, but the purpose of the operation is to use this knowledge in order to reveal the code so that we can apply it to events in the future that we do not know by any other means. We leave, as we always will, the old letters in their correct positions above the modern versions of them. The reasons for this will become clear.

In this version, the verse is transformed into straightforward simple prose. One of the two major reasons why Nostradamus' prophecies have always appeared incoherent is the fact that interpreters always went directly for the verses. The tension between these two forms, the visible verse and the hidden prose, creates the confusion for the reader. The other principal reason for confusion will become clear with further examples. Before we get into the actual decoding method we must go deeper into these examples. The reader is requested simply to trust the method for the moment.

So what does this new form of the prediction offer us?

Firstly, it offers a much more complete picture of the event. Continuity is often lacking in any prophecy, but we may suspect that those of Nostradamus and certainly older forms of prophecy, such as those appearing in the Bible, mutilated any form of continuity to avoid detection at awkward times. As a Jew, Nostradamus is simply following a very ancient tradition of his forebears. The repositioning of the words, therefore, offers an opportunity to return to the original prophecy hidden behind the distorted verse.

Secondly, there are the details, always present, often pointed out, but usually, in the verses, not presented with any clarity. In this new prose form everything is very clear.

Henry's opponent, Montgomery, was younger than the King. The lion was an emblem used by Henry. The tournament field could be described as a "warlike field" without actually being a field of war. Montgomery's lance would blind the King in one eye.

Next comes the amazing description "Eyes in a Golden cage" – a reference to Henry himself, *since he was wearing a gilt helmet with a barred visor.*

The phrase "deux classes" can be identified with "training runs", meaning the two previous jousts with Montgomery, before the third in which Henry was fatally wounded.

Nevertheless, despite all the glorious drama of the verse, its exciting imagery deludes us into thinking that it conveys more than it really does. There is not one single hard fact, one name, one date which could be drawn from this prediction to establish the accuracy of Nostradamus. That is not a satisfactory situation and one of the main reasons why so many people have become somewhat cynical about Nostradamus' predictions – how can we believe something that can be interpreted in so many different ways?

The details of the prophecy caused a storm when they were known in Paris. Calls came from the Inquisition authorities for Nostradamus to be arrested for questioning. His effigy burned in the streets.

Perhaps the Prophet was somewhat protected by the influence of Catherine, but had the true meaning of the prophecy been known, Nostradamus could not have escaped torture and the stake. He knew too much. In fact, he knew even more than the authorities suspected.

In order to illustrate this extraordinary degree of knowledge we can look at the first line of the prophecy.

Le jeune surmontera le vieux lion In English –
   "The young man will overcome the old lion"
   Now look at it again transformed.

Le jeune Mont(gomery) rusera le lion vieux
"The young Mont(gomery) will deceive the old lion"

Everything is the same, except that the verb "surmontera" has become "Mont rusera" – "Mont" will deceive.

The most startling aspect of this transformation is the emergence of part of the name *Montgomery*. This is evidence that Nostradamus knew before the event who the protagonist was going to be. Remember that the prophecy was published four years before the event.

The second piece of information is that he not only "overcomes", but deceives "the old lion".

Does this merely refer to his ability to deceive the king in the joust, so piercing the royal defense and by a terrible misfortune fatally wounding Henry?

Or does it indicate a deliberate intention or even a conspiracy to kill Henry?

Although it was thought at the time to be an accident, later events cast a doubt. Henry had been particularly zealous and cruel in persecuting the Protestant Huguenots of France. Many had been hideously tortured and executed. Montgomery was Scottish, a land where Protestantism was burgeoning fast.

Soon after Henry died, Montgomery left France, but he returned seventeen years later as a leader in a Huguenot uprising. He was captured and put to death by Catherine de Medici in Paris. Was there a stronger reason than simple revenge for Catherine's insistence that Montgomery should die? Henry II, after all, had pardoned him before he died. Nostradamus tells us that there was. Who is "the old lion"? Let's take another look at this line.

> *Le jeune Mont(gomery) rusera le lion vieux*
> This then becomes:

> **i   u   l   y**
> *Le jeune Mont(gomery) rue Henri Rex Valois*
> "The young Mont(gomery) attacks Henry, the Valois King."

The complete meaning of the line therefore is: "The young man will overcome the old lion. The young Mont(gomery) will deceive the old lion. He attacks Henry the Valois King."

Henry, the "Valois King", is revealed as the other duelist. If we look at the original line of the prophecy, we see that it contains an anagram, making "surmontera" into "Mont rusera", so that we

When Nostradamus gave his private prophesies to Catherine he was very careful as to what he might reveal to the strong willed and often dangerous queen. He could hardly tell her outright that her entire family would not survive her so he concealed his predictions in difficult verses. Now we can see just how accurate he was.

might realize that there is likely to be more of this kind of shenanigans in the same text.

There are four letters appearing above the line. The letter "i" was the old letter in the original "ieune".

The letter "y" appeared in "lyon" and was pushed upwards by the modern "i". Although "lyon/lion" has now disappeared from the new line, the old letter "y" must still be kept above the letter "i" as this will help us to define the date of the prediction.

The substitute "y" is in Valois, not in Henry. A crucial principle of the system is that only one substitute letter may appear in any word. Henry already has a substitute letter – "u". The only other "i" in the new prediction occurs in Valois.

"U" and "i" were present in the line – *Mont(gomery) rusera le lion vieux*. They must be kept to date the text, even though they are not now part of the new line.

So the method is to "dig out" the new text by treating it as an anagram and rearrange the letters in keeping with the information given in the prophecy and include what we know of the historical event.

i   u   l   y
j   h   r   i

These are the four substitute letters (the letters on the top line) and the letters which have replaced them on the second line. The most obvious point to notice is the word "iuly" or July. The letters "I" and "J" obtain the same numerical value (as we shall see in the Numerical Code later in this section) – 10.

Henry II died on the 10th July 1559.

So now we must take a look at the dating system.

HOW TO USE THE DATING SYSTEM

The system is founded on two principles –

1. – the Numeric Alphabet in which each letter has its own number and

2. – the Substituted Letter Device in which the numbers belonging to the "raised" letters in a line of the text, together with the numbers of the new letters immediately below the raised letters are analysed for dates which support and extend the meaning of the new predictions.

3. – A third aspect of the system is the "time-signal" explained below.

THE NUMERIC ALPHABET

This is made up of the 24 letters of the old French alphabet, excluding the Greek "k" and the Germanic "w", neither of which appear in modern French. Each letter has its own number.

a	b	c	d	e	f	g	h	i	j	l	m	n	o	p	q	r	s	t	u	v	x	y	z
1	2	3	4	5	6	7	8	9	10	11	12	13	14	15	16	17	18	19	20	21	22	23	24

In the text, the letter "k" is substituted by "c" and "w" by "uu" or double-u.

ROMAN NUMERALS

Three letters also possess numbers from the Latin or Roman numbering system.

I = one, V = five and X = ten.

This is particularly important for "I", whose two values 1 and 9 often apply to predictions of this century.

THE NUMBER 10.

By itself, the number 10 can also signify 1, 1 and 9 (making 10), or even on occasion 19 (1 and 9 again making 10).

NUMBER REDUCTION

Numbers ending in zero can be reduced by deducting the zero. 10 – 1, 20 = 2 etc.

The number 11 attached to letter "L" may be reduced to 2. In most cases either 11 is reduced to one:one for use in the calculation, or if that does not seem to produce relevant information, it is reduced to 2.

NUMERICAL ANAGRAMS

Numerical anagrams are sets of mixed up numbers which emerge from these substitute letter devices in the lines of secret prophecy, which then have to be decoded.

TIME-SIGNALS AND TIME WORDS

Time-words are normal French words, woven inconspicuously into the text of the predictions. They are all words whose meaning is linked with an aspect of time.

Typical examples are "jour/day", "jeune/young" and "encore/again".

Such words in the predictions betray the presence of a date, or series of dates related to the subject of the text. Other words, such as those connected with rank or royalty, often contain dating aspects.

OTHER INFORMATION

A letter/number can signify other information, such as royal lines of descent – Charles the Second, or George the Sixth. Numbers can either be used as they are: 11, 12, 13 etc., or "reduced" by adding them together – 18 = 9, 16 = 7 and so on.

Dating and other numerical information will appear throughout this book under the heading – TIME-SIGNALS.

The reader will find when studying the dating system that the same dates will be confirmed several times through a variety of calculations and different numbers, thus discounting the possibility of simple coincidence.

As a brief practical example we can take a look at the time-signal of the verse we have examined in this section.

TIME-SIGNAL – Prophecy I.35 Line one.

```
i    u    l    y
j    h    r    i
```

The first thing to notice about this arrangement of letters is that the top four letters very nearly represent the word "July".

The missing "J" is the first letter of the lower set.

As will be seen throughout the pages of the book, this kind of formation happens too often to be coincidence, it is the result of the correct application of the decoding system. Henry II dies during July 10th. English words appear from time to time in the secret prophecies. Under the dating system, both letter "i" and "j" are worth 10. So let us dig a little deeper into this collection of letters by setting out their numbers. It must be noted here that we are, of course, deducing the dating system by working backwards from dates that we already have. Again, we are cheating! But it will become clear that this is merely a method which will later allow us to apply the same system to the future.

```
i    u    l    y        1:9   20   11   23
j    h    r    i        10    8    17   1:9
```

These eight numbers hold the dating of the event described by the Prophecy I.35

```
i          1:9
j          10
```
9-1-1 = 7 = the 7th month, July.

July – the month when Henry died – appears in the letters belonging to this set.

```
u     20 + 8 = 28
h     8 – 2 = 6 = the 6th month, June
```
The tournament in which Henry was fatally wounded began on the 28th June.
```
l        11
r        17
```
7 + 1 + 1 + 1 – 10 = 10th day of July (7)

Henry died on the 10th July.
```
y        23      =   5
i        1:9     =   1   9
```

CHARLES IX *(8 years old)*

CHARLES IX *(23 years old)*

Charles IX. Henry's son, called the "savage", or worse, the "black", was a cruel and hated king. He sanctioned the hideous St. Bartholomew's Day Massacre of the Huguenots. It was with considerable public relief that he expired at the age of 24 from a common cold.

The year of the prophecy is 1559

The final confirmation occurs in the letter device in the name of Henri in the prediction.

u   = 20   = 2

henri

The device confirms that the Valois King called Henri whom Nostradamus refers to in the prediction is Henry the Second.

The period of the time-signal is 28th June – 10th July. The tournament opened on 28th June and Henry died on the 10th July.

"Jeune" is a time-word describing Montgomery.

```
j  e  u                n   e
10 5  20              13   5
10 5 + 2 = 7
10         7   =   10th July
```

The left set provides the vital date of the King's death yet again – further confirmation.

The right set is even more remarkable – 13 and 5 appear as the decoded numbers from the two raised letters "n" and "e". 135 is also the verse number. Perhaps this is Nostradamus' complex seal of approval for our solution to the riddle.

So, having run through the total "package" on this verse, we end up with, including dating:

"The young Montgomery attacks Henry the Second, the Valois King, during the period 28th June - 10th July 1559."

If we think back to the original image of the "Vulcan" and his furnace – the image that Nostradamus gave us in his Preface – we can now experience the device first hand – the methods by which he distorted his verses artificially in order to disguise his genius from those whom he knew would not be equipped to accept it. Now that we begin to "melt down" this extraordinary raw material, we find that perhaps we can reconstruct the original prose prophecy – allowing the prophecy to emerge from its hiding place amongst the lines of the verse.

BY SINGULAR DUEL

To give further confirmation of the method to be used in the book we can complete line two of the prophecy.

En champ bellique par singulier duelle
– using anagramatic techniques becomes –

b　　**i**　　　　**l**

que le chapelet ne lie pas (Mont)gomeri, dur nul — retaining the old letters above becomes then in English —
"as the rosary does not bind (Mont)gomery, the harsh man (is) no more."

Here the intermediate stages of coding have not been included to save space, but the reader can test them if required, using the previously explained system. The most important point is to look for anything that appears unusual. "Duel" is "duelle" in Nostradamus' lines — aberrant spelling gives us a hint that a different prediction is concealed in the text. The "singulier" gives us a last syllable — "lier" which is also the French verb "to bind." By these detective methods we can find the true meaning of the lines.

Nostradamus regarded Montgomery as Henry's assassin. His name emerges in line one and in line two we learn more about the situation. By the time of the making of the prediction, Gabriel Lorges, Comte de Montgomery, Captain of Henry II's Scottish Guard, was no longer a Catholic. The rosary is the portable image of Roman Catholicism — the single most familiar object within the faith. Thus we have — "As the rosary does not bind Montgomery, the harsh man is no more..." The tournament was a perfect opportunity for Montgomery to avenge the Protestants and prevent Henry from committing further crimes against them. As can be seen in the time-signal, the dates are yet again confirmed using the same code.

TIME-SIGNAL Prophecy I.35, line two —

	b	i	l	2	1:9	11
	e	t	o	5	19	14

The number 11 is reduced to 2 before calculation.

2		10		2
5		10		14
2 + 5 = 7	10	10		2 + 1 + 4 = 7

The date emerges as 10th July, twice!

Passing on now briefly to the last two lines of the verse we can conclude our testing phase.

With Line 3 we see the consequences of this act.

y

les yeux dans cage d'or lui crevera
becomes

CATHERINE DE 'MEDICI

HENRY III

Catherine lived to see all her sons die before her. By the time Henry III reached the throne she was forced to relinquish her power as Regent. Henry, a universally unpopular, homosexual ruler, was assassinated by a Franciscan monk called Clement, thus ending the royal line of the Valois.

l   y   d   c

(Mont)gomery a rasé u = 20; casque henri X du leve
"(Mont)gomery has brought down the "Second". The helmet raises the indebted Henry."

The Protestant Henry IV who was proclaimed King in 1589 was, in Nostradamus' eyes, historically indebted to Henry II's killer, since it brought about his own succession through the infertility and early death of Henry's sons. (The crossed poles of the letter X uncrossed to signify 11 or 2 is a device often used by Nostradamus to denote royal titles.)

Henry IV was forced to fight for his kingdom before it would yield to him. It was not until 1593 that he was able to enter Paris – hence the reference to his soldier's helmet.

In line three of the verse a rare past tense occurs. This section of the prophecy has now moved past Henry's death in 1559 and concentrates on its historical consequences – the succession of Henry IV, first of the Bourbon line thirty years later.

That succession changed the future of the world, for it brought about the French Revolution and shaped much of modern politics until the East European revolutions in 1989.

The final line of the prophecy contains the most remarkable information so far.

v

Deux classes une puis mourir mort cruelle
becomes

s   s   p   u   s   u   r

Mort – seul loue a Caterina Medici, veuve, Rex 1 = 2.
"Dead, the one man hired by Catherine de Medici, widow of the King, who is the second."

We may notice the number of substitute letters in this last line – as though Nostradamus wished to securely hide this treasonable message from everyone! This is not surprising as he appears to be saying that Catherine de Medici was herself involved in the assassination of her husband Henry II.

Catherine used Montgomery as her political instrument.

Catherine had borne her husband seven children, including four sons, during the twenty-four years of her marriage. She was a short,

MARY QUEEN OF SCOTS

Nostradamus precisely predicted when the sickly Francis would die and foretold that Mary Stuart, his wife, would be childless. When the King died just before his eighteenth birthday the Spanish Ambassador wrote to Phillip II "These catastrophes have struck the court with stupor, together with the warning of Nostradamus, who it would be better to punish than to allow to sell his prophecies, which lead to vain and superstitious beliefs."

FRANCIS II

dumpy, plain woman, whereas her rival, the King's mistress, Diane de Poitiers, was a legendary beauty and wit, rumored to maintain the King's interest in her by aphrodisiacs and enchantments.

Catherine had often been slighted in this woman's presence, treated as if she were ranked behind her.

But in 1558 an event had taken place which might have set Catherine's mind working on a way to change that state of affairs. Her eldest son Francis had married the young Mary Queen of Scots.

Since Henry had fathered seven legitimate children, she had no reason to suspect that Francis would have any difficulty. Mary was a charming, healthy girl.

By 1559 the entire Court would have known of the three-year-old prediction from her Italian astrologer in 1556, confirmed by Nostradamus in the same year and communicated to Henry himself that he would face blindness and death in his forty-first year.

When the tournament came, could it have been possible that Catherine used Montgomery as her instrument of assassination? Her reputation for intrigue is the most famous in history.

She could trust in her ability to manipulate the teenagers Francis and Mary, rather than the autocratic, harsh Henry who had been in love with another woman for years.

This is the scenario which the last line of the secret prophecy appears to suggest.

When Montgomery returned to France years later to lead a Huguenot rebellion, he was captured and put to death by Catherine's troops in Paris.

By then, Catherine's third son, Henry III, was ruler. She was no longer Regent of France and the folly of a past act might have been very perilous to her then, had the truth come out.

Montgomery, the one man who knew the truth, had to be eliminated.

"Dead – the one man hired by Catherine de Medici, widow of the King."

We can now see perhaps more clearly just how much more complex and fascinating Nostradamus' prophecies are. And this is only the beginning for all we have done in this short demonstration is to decode the basic information from the naked lines of the verse. We haven't yet looked behind the lines into the deeper and almost magical material that lies there.

THE FINAL CODE

NTIL THIS POINT IN THE BOOK, we have understood hopefully the method by which verses can be used to decode the past, the present and the future — using verses that *start* in our past. We have been standing on more or less firm ground. But now we need to lose our footing altogether and in order to do this there is a refinement to the coding system that must be added.

In order to illustrate the refinement we will take verse III.65 once again to illustrate the last refinement of the system. The following decoded and anagrammatically melted-down prediction concerns the future directly and Europe in the form of Rome, in particular. Close attention is needed to understand the new refinement of the coding system.

```
c                          p                            j
Karol mourra quand l'Europe a l'est du Rhin, Russie seront devenus piles
                    s           y    p       a  i  f
Age des guerres tue un fer voue. Apres an/ de sac, Rome nuee; cloches/ne
        p        i
sonnent. / Age
```

"Karol will pass away when Europe to the east of the Rhine and Russia have reversed their coin. An age of wars kills the consecrated iron man. After a year of pillage, Rome stripped bare; the bells no longer ring. Age — "

In this case we give the time-signal material in full —

Time-Signal

c	p	j	s		y	p	a	i	f	p	i
k	e	s	f		d	r	e	c	e	t	Age
3	15	10	18		23	15	1	1:9	6	15	1:9
	5	18	6		4	17	5	3	5	19	175
3	6	1	9	1	5	6	1	19	6	6	19
	5	9	6	9	4	8	5	3	5	19	1 7 5
	9	91		Dec			Jan		6	196	195
	5	96		94		8	5	193	May		Jan7 or Oct 7.

The meltdown reveals much. First we are told that the Pope – Karol Wojtyla – will pass away in 1995. By that year Russia and the other countries of Eastern Europe will have become market economies. Between 1991 - 1995 there will be a period of conflict involving Rome which will result in the Pope's death. "Europe to the east of the Rhine" includes much of Germany – her postwar capital has been Bonn, which lies on the River Rhine, but perhaps Nostradamus is telling us that once the east and west are merged in a unified Germany, the new capital will once again be Berlin. This would be an apt result of the greater involvement of Western

Germany with her new partner.

Rome will be overrun and looted of her religious treasures between 5th January 1993 and 8th December 1994. Christian churches will not ring their bells on the 6th May 1996. We may assume from this that Christian worship will have ceased, at least temporarily, from that point.

From the time-signal we can pin down the date of the Pope's death as being either January 7th or October 7th of 1995. 7th October is the more likely date as the number 75 appears in the final device and the Pope will reach the age of 75 on the 18th May 1995 – after January 7th.

We will see in other parts of the book that this is a serious and disruptive period for Rome, Italy and countries around the Mediterranean. Commercial shipping in this part of the world is disturbed through conflicts in the south of Europe.

When this verse was first melted down, it appeared to be concerned largely with the existing Pope but also seemed to contain some detail surrounding his life and death. However, as time passed it became clear that there was much more embedded in the verse than this. A whole panoramic vista is opened up by the verse – as though Nostradamus were using these seemingly simple lines to paint a wide picture of the whole state of Europe. Once again, the opening of the Pandora's box revealed an entire nest of goodies. When the initial decoding was done, the changes in Europe and Russia had only just started – the reunification of Germany had not even begun at that time and yet the details were there, lying beneath the surface – staring us in the face! Nostradamus was giving us what he saw as an established fact – the reunification of Germany – to indicate the prospected changes that would take place in the whole of Europe and Russia.

And here we can begin to see the final requirement for predicting the future. The secret is to "key in" certain vital words on a given subject in order to get back details of events in the future.

Using the now familiar verse – III.65 – we chose the following words as our key to the future –

Karol mourra – "Karol will die."

The device, of course, depends somewhat on the instinct of the "operator" for what is important as a feature of prediction. The Pope is clearly a major figure in today's political, social and religious events and so his death must also figure as a substantial feature of change in the future. It would seem therefore to be a vital key to changes to come. Also, the event has not yet occurred. If the prophecy, Nostradamus' original quatrain, has anything to say on the subject of the Pope's death it would have to be speaking to us of our future. The result of this was truly spectacular. The prediction called *The Sack of Rome* – a dramatic title for a dramatic result, for the keying in of this important event – the death of the Pope – opened up a panoramic vista of the way the world will look at the time of this event.

Just like unlocking a door into a fantastic world, our keying-in process takes us through the door as though we really were time travelers – the resulting picture a whole world of hitherto unknown information.

So – to summarize this last but most important feature of the prediction code – we take the key words from the melted-down prophecy – in this case *Karol mourra* – and isolate them. What remains of the four-line verse makes up the rest of the new prediction. If we were to take the words *Nations Unis* instead, we would then find a different prediction which relates to the United Nations involvement in the future. If we wanted instead to find out about George Bush, we would take the letters that make up his name and then the rest of the prophecy would give us the answers surrounding the US president.

Each verse functions as an oracle – with all the twists and turns traditionally resulting from an oracle – the answers very often not being those that we might wish to receive! Keying in the question and then abiding by the rules of the hitherto explained system will inevitably result in answers that give us accurate views of our future. One more addition to be made before we proceed to use the oracle extensively –

MODIFICATION OF THE FUTURE DATING SYSTEM

Dating from prophecies that have already occurred is obviously not difficult as we have the events to verify our instinct and the system we have adopted. Dating into an unknown future is somewhat of a different matter. The system for this, however, is only a slight adaptation of the original system.

To reach a time-signal and a precise date for the future, we must first decode the prediction using all the letters within the prophecy. When we have used up all the letters there will still remain a number of substitute letters which appear at certain points above the lines of the text. These and the letters immediately below them form the basis for our dating system. So far, this is familiar.

However, when we have extracted a prediction clearly describing our future, how can we adopt the dating system so that it will offer us dates in the future which might be seen to apply to the new prediction? Let us look back at the time-signal which we displayed at the beginning of this prediction and explanation section. It is repeated on this page with some additional features of explanation —

Time-Signal

c	p	j	s		y	p	a	i	f	p	i
k	e	s	f		d	r	e	c	e	t	Age
3	15	10	18		23	15	1	1:9	6	15	1:9
	5	18	6		4	17	5	3	5	19	175
3	6	1	9	1	5	6	1	19	6	6	19
	5	9	6	9	4	8	5	3	5	19	1 7 5
	9	91		Dec			Jan		6	196	195
	5	96		94		8	5	193	May		Jan7 or Oct 7.

The vital clue in this case is the frequent appearance of the numbers 9 and 19 in the time-signal chart. We have dropped the numbers of the letters down to a second row by adding together the two-digit numbers. For instance – 15 becomes 6, 23 becomes 5, 17 becomes 8 and so on. When 18 is added together it becomes 9 – one of the special numbers which helps us to reveal year dates. Single digit numbers remain as they are. 1:9 becomes 19 on the dropped row.

We can immediately figure out that the "year" aspects of our dating emerge from the numbers 9 and 19. We then, as the second stage, divide up the dates into sections – trying always to keep track of the sense of the text as we do so. The dates and the words work in harmony to produce greater information. There can be no separation of the two, after all, they only occur in tandem – time and space.

When calculating the year 2000 or 2001 there will be separate notes to the predictions to explain the device.

But still, the system cannot obviously be verified until events start to come true. We are therefore still at a primitive stage of decoding and will remain so until the period of monitoring begins with the publication of this book. This whole process is, by its very nature, is still experimental for everyone using or reading it. It may appear on occasion that arbitrary rules have been applied for slicing up the date cake, but we have to start somewhere for the future really is an infinite dimension. Either we slice somewhere at random or we get no slices at all!

SUPPLEMENTARY DATES.

Inevitably there are one or two restrictions to this "drop-line" system. Since all the numbers result in single digits, except 19, the months November and December (11 and 12) cannot be decoded. Nor can the dates of the month from 11 - 31. The tenth month, October, and the 10th day of the month arise from extending 1 into 10 – this is permissible under the existing code rules.

To go some way towards solving this enigma the original two rows of numbers have been reincluded at the middle of the time-signal as "Supplementary Dates". These include all the original double-date numbers. We can therefore pick out 15th May, 18th October, 23rd April and 19th March as being related to the prediction. The highest day-date number, however, can only ever be 24 as there are only this many letters in the alphabet. Thus we are still left with the day-dates between 25-31 unaccounted for. The only method we can assume for solving this problem is by accepting that on occasions where there are two numbers we simply add them together to get the appropriate dates – 23 and 4, for example, giving us the 27th of the month.

Ultimately, however, when attempting to decode Nostradamus with some perfection we are reliant on one factor – trust, until some of the events have begun to be fulfilled. The authors have tested the scheme to their own satisfaction using the methods on events in their future which have now been fulfilled. But the readers can only do this once the book has reached their hands and been given time to prove itself. Gaps will be filled and further volumes will follow as the system is authenticated.

To my mother for the early years.

ACKNOWLEDGEMENTS

The authors would like to thank everyone at Labyrinth Publishing and of course the Master Nostradamus himself with grateful respect and affection to him who is always one step ahead.

CREDITS

The Publishers would like to thank the following Photographic Agencies for their help in locating photographs: Frank Spooner, Art Directors, Gamma, Popperphoto, Environmental Library, Associated Press, Magnum, REX Features and Zefa.

Photographs:
24/5 G. Kearle, 36/7 Pascal Maitre, 40/1 NASA, 44/5 Lochon, 50/1 Eric Bouvet, 54/5 Patrick Piel, 57/8 *Sunday Times*, 60/1/2/3 Daniel Velez, 65 Iverson (Time), 66 David Rubinger (Time), 68/9 Baitel, 70/1 Patrick Baz, 83 Kerman, 88/9 Don James, 90/1 Bartholomew, 98/9 E. Sander, 106/7 Vlastinir Shone, 109 Evening Standard, 110/11 Syndication International, 112 C. Vioujard, 112/13 Mark Deville, 114 Dave Lewis, 115 Robin Platzer, 116 Peter Magubane, 117 Bernet, 118/19 Barry King, 120/21 Rick Diamond, 122/3 Udo Weitz, 136/37 Chuck O'Rear, 137 Maggie Steber, 138/39 Sarjkano, 142/43 Ansin, 147 Oldfield, 154/55 Alex Olaa, 156/57 Eliot Elisofon, 158/9 Eric Bouvet, 160/1 Marc Riboud, 165 Arkek Katie, 164 A. De Wildeburg, 167 Oswald Iten, 168 M. Manson, 170/71 Syndication International, 172 Julian Parker, 173 V. Miles.